MW00625796

WASHINGTON
COOK BOOK

by

Janet Walker
Everett, Washington

**GOLDEN
WEST ☼
PUBLISHERS**

Cover photo by Dick Dietrich

Printed in the United States of America

6th printing © 2001

ISBN #0-914846-97-3

Copyright © 1994 by Golden West Publishers. All rights reserved. This book, or any portion thereof, may not be reproduced in any form, except for review purposes without the written permission of the publisher.

Information in this book is deemed to be authentic and accurate by editor and publisher. However, they disclaim any liability incurred in connection with the use of information appearing in this book.

Golden West Publishers
4113 N. Longview Ave.
Phoenix, AZ 85014, USA
(602) 265-4392

Introduction

Ah, Washington! Here are the panoramic deep canyons with rushing streams, the towering majestic mountains, the dense rain forests, the fertile valleys, and the shimmering bays and coast lines! Yes, and here, too, are the spreading sagebrushed plains, the rolling wheatlands, and the highly productive farmlands that provide such bountiful crops!

Dividing Washington (66,511 square miles, 20th largest in the U.S.), is the Cascade Range — jagged, snowy, rugged and tall (Mt. Rainier is 14,411 ft.). Other high peaks are Mount Adams, Glacier Peak and the always white Mount Baker. Once, the almost perfectly cone-shaped Mount St. Helens was among the tallest, before the May, 1980 catastrophic eruption reduced her to 8,364 feet.

Washington produces more delicious and juicy, bright red and yellow apples than any other state in the union. Other orchard fruit crops include cherries, peaches, pears, nectarines and plums. The fertile valleys also produce berries, peas, potatoes, lettuce, asparagus, beans, and onions as well as hops, flower bulbs and seeds. Grapes have made Washington second only to California in the production of vinifera wine. Dairying and beef cattle, as well as lumber industries, are also important to the state's economy. Tourism ranks as the fourth largest industry in the state.

This scenic state leads the West Coast in the processing and distribution of seafoods, claiming more than 200 edible species. Salmon, of course, are among the most prized. Much of the halibut caught in cold Alaskan waters are processed in the Puget Sound region. Such delicacies as Hood Canal or Willapa Bay oysters, Dungeness crab and razor or geoduck clams are abundant.

These recipes offer your palate the opportunity to savor the delicacies for which this glorious state has become famous. Here are some highly prized recipes from ordinary citizens like you and me, as well as from some of the state's famous dignitaries. You will also find carefully-guarded recipes from some of the most popular eateries, featuring Ellensburg lamb and beef, Yakima corn and tomatoes, Puyallup rhubarb, cucumbers and berries, Walla Walla onions, Wenatchee and Yakima apples, chicken from the Dutch-themed town of Lynden, mussels from picturesque Whidbey Island, potatoes from Mount Vernon or Moses Lake and chanterelle mushrooms from the slopes of Mount Rainier.

Enjoy with us a "Bite of Washington"

Acknowledgments

We would like to gratefully express our thanks to so many helpful Washingtonians who assisted us by contributing their recipes. These include many of Washington's finest restaurants, food manufacturers, and bed-and-breakfast establishments.

Particularly, we thank our Governor Mike Lowry, our two Senators Slade Gorton and Patty Murray, Congressman Al Swift, and Seattle Mayor Norm Rice.

In compiling trivia for this publication, we are indebted to the State of Washington Tourism Division, The Apple Growers of Washington and The Washington Apple Commission. We sincerely appreciate your help in the preparation of *The Washington Cook Book!*

Table of Contents

Northwestern Seafood

Side Dishes

Breads

Desserts

Beverages

Recipe Contributors

'37 House B & B
4B's Restaurants
Albatross B & B
American Fine Foods
Apple Growers of Wash. State
Arnie's Restaurants
Campbell's Resort
Canlis Restaurant
Campbell House
Captain Whidbey Inn
Collector's Choice Rest.
Downey House B & B
Edgewater Inn
Fowler, Chris
Fowler, Joyce
Fraine, Betty
Gorton, Slade, U. S. Sen.
Hayes, Evelyn
Hillhouse, Melva

Holeman, Jimmie
Holton, Mae
Inn of the White Salmon
James House B & B
Janot's Bistro
Johnny's Dock Rest.
Kain, Laura
Kerr, Graham
Knaus, Randi
Knudson, Gary James
Knudson, Jennifer
Knudson, Phillip
Lowry, Mike, Gov. of Wash.
Moon and Sixpence B & B
Mt. Rainier Guest Services
Murray, Patty, U. S. Senator
Nalley's Fine Foods
Nielsen, Debbie
Ocean Crest Dinner House

Orcas Hotel
Rice, Norman B., Mayor
   of Seattle
Shelburne Inn
Simone's Groveland
   Cottage B & B
Sun Mountain Lodge
Swift, Al, Congressman-U. S.
   House of Rep.
Thorne, Sister Mary
Turtleback Farm Inn
Twickenham House B & B
Walker, Brittany
Walker, James
Walker, Jerry & Lisa
Walker, Tracey
Walker, Rev. Willis
Washington Apple Comm.
Watson, Opal

Washington Facts

Size—20th largest state in area

Statehood—November 11, 1889

Highest Elevation—Mount Rainier, 14,410'

Lowest Elevation—Pacific Ocean, sea level

Highest Temperature—118 degrees

Lowest Temperature—48 degrees below zero

Land in Farms—16,000,000 acres

Named For—George Washington, only state named for a president. 42nd State admitted to the Union

State Motto—"Alki", an Indian word meaning "bye and bye"

State Nickname— "The Evergreen State"

State Bird—The Willow Goldfinch (or Wild Canary)

State Fruit—The apple, adopted in 1989

State Tree—The Western Hemlock, adopted in 1947

State Flower—The Coast Rhododendron (1892)

State Gem—Petrified wood, adopted in 1975

State Fish—Steelhead trout (1969)

Washington Tourist Information

Washington State Board of Tourism
101 General Administration Building
Olympia, WA 98504-2500 — 800-544-1800

Anacortes Chamber of Commerce	206-293-3832
Dayton Chamber of Commerce	800-882-6299
East King County Visitors Bureau	800-252-1926
Ephrata Chamber of Commerce	800-345-4656
Moses Lake Chamber of Commerce	800-992-6234
Omak Visitor Information Center	800-225-OMAK
Pullman Chamber of Commerce	800-ENJOY IT
Puyallup Chamber of Commerce	800-634-2334
Tacoma Visitors Bureau	800-272-2662
Tri Cities Visitor Bureau	800-666-1929
Westport Chamber of Commerce	800-345-6223
Washington State Ferries	800-84-FERRY

Appetizers

Warm Crab Dip

U. S. Senator and Mrs. Slade Gorton

1 pkg. (8 oz.) CREAM CHEESE, softened at room temperature
1/4 cup MILK
1 Tbsp. MAYONNAISE
2 Tbsp. CHILI SAUCE
3 drops TABASCO® SAUCE
2 Tbsp. ONION, onion
1/2 tsp. SALT
1 cup CRAB MEAT, cooked (Dungeness preferred)
3 Tbsp. GREEN OLIVES, sliced
1 can (8 1/2 oz.) ARTICHOKES (not marinated), coarsely chopped

Preheat oven to 375 degrees. In a mixing bowl, combine all ingredients except crab, olives and artichokes. Mix thoroughly, and then, gently fold in the remaining ingredients. Spread into an 8 inch baking dish. Bake for 15 minutes. Serve while hot, along with crackers or corn chips. Serves 8.

"Elegant, yet quick and simple to prepare."

Hot Crab & Artichoke Dip

Arnie's Restaurants — Mukilteo, Edmonds and Seattle

1 lb. CREAM CHEESE
4 cups MAYONNAISE
1 1/2 lb. DUNGENESS CRAB, drained well
2 cups ARTICHOKE HEARTS, quartered
1 cup WHITE ONIONS, diced
1/4 tsp. WHITE PEPPER
1/2 tsp. TABASCO®
1/2 tsp. SHERRY VINEGAR
1 tsp. GARLIC, minced
1/4 cup GREEN ONIONS, minced
1/4 cup RED PEPPERS, minced
1/4 cup CELERY, minced
1 Tbsp. PARSLEY, chopped
6 cups GRATED PARMESAN CHEESE

In mixer, whip cream cheese until soft, but not airy. Then fold in all remaining ingredients, adding cheese last. Bake in 375 degree oven for 10 minutes until lightly browned on top and bubbling around the edges. Serve with toasted crouton rounds.

Light Fantastic Spinach Dip

Nalley's Fine Foods — Tacoma

1/2 pkg. DRY SPINACH SOUP MIX
1 cup NON-FAT YOGURT
1/2 cup BERNSTEINS LIGHT FANTASTIC® RANCH
    SALAD DRESSING
1 GREEN ONION, chopped
2 Tbsp. PARSLEY, finely chopped

Combine all ingredients; cover and chill for one hour. Stir and serve with raw vegetables, tortilla chips or mixed grain chips. For a spicy dip, add **1/2 jalapeño pepper**, seeded and finely minced.

> *Since being founded in 1918 by Marcus Nalley, Nalley's Fine Foods of "Nalley Valley" has constantly produced uniformly high quality food products.*

Original Penn Cove Mussels

Captain Whidbey Inn — Coupeville

4 Tbsp. FRESH BASIL, chopped
1 cup DRY WHITE WINE
4 Tbsp. BUTTER
2 lbs. MUSSELS, cleaned and de-bearded

Combine basil, wine and butter in large saucepan. Add mussels and cover pan. Steam over medium heat until mussels open (about 5 minutes). Discard any mussels which do not open. Serve in individual bowls with some of the "nectar" from the pan, and french bread. The nectar is wonderful for dipping the bread!

Some of the world's finest mussels are produced in the crystal blue waters of Penn Cove at Captain Whidbey Inn. Each March, a full four days are set aside to honor the mollusk at the Penn Cove Mussel Festival. There's something for everyone: cooking demonstrations by well-known chefs, tips on mussel farming, lots of mussels to eat and cruises on the Inn's 52-foot ketch, the Cutty Sark.

Spicy Clam Dip

1/4 cup MARGARINE, melted
1 sm. ONION, diced
1/2 GREEN PEPPER, diced
1/4 lb. PROCESSED CHEESE
1/4 cup CATSUP
TABASCO® to taste
2 cans CLAMS, drained

Using the melted margarine, sauté the onion and pepper until tender. Stir in the cheese, catsup, Tabasco and clams. Heat until the cheese is melted. Serve hot with your favorite cracker.

Trout Dip

Randi Knaus, The Herald — Everett

1 pkg. (8 oz.) CREAM CHEESE
1/2 cup MAYONNAISE
GARLIC POWDER to taste
COARSE GROUND PEPPER to taste
2 GREEN ONIONS, sliced
1/2 fillet SMOKED TROUT

Mix the cream cheese and mayonnaise together (a few lumps are okay.) Add garlic powder and pepper. Gently fold in the green onions and trout.

Afternoon Apple Snacks

Mike Lowry, Governor - State of Washington — Olympia

2 RED DELICIOUS APPLES
LEMON JUICE
1/2 cup CHUNKY PEANUT BUTTER
2 Tbsp. HONEY
1/2 tsp. GROUND CINNAMON
6 whole GRAHAM CRACKERS

Core the apples, cut each in half. Cut each half into 3 wedges to make a total of 12 wedges. Dip wedges in lemon juice to keep apples from turning brown, and place in a single layer in a microwave on high for 3-1/2 to 4 minutes, until apples are tender, but hold their shape. Drain on paper towels. In a small bowl, combine peanut butter, honey and cinnamon. Snap graham crackers in half to make 12 square crackers. Place 2 apple wedges on 6 square crackers, and spread a layer of peanut butter mixture on apples. Top with remaining cracker squares to make sandwiched snacks.

When passing through Olympia, you can't help but notice the capitol building. Its design closely resembles the Acropolis in Athens, Greece. Close in design to the U. S. Capitol in Washington, D.C., it was first occupied by the Washington Legislature in 1927.

Spicy Sautéed Shrimp Appetizer

Sun Mountain Lodge — Winthrop

1 lb. (21-25) SHRIMP
2 oz. OLIVE OIL
1 tsp. GARLIC
3 oz. OYSTER MUSHROOMS
3 oz. WHITE WINE
3/4 oz. LEMON JUICE
1/2 tsp. PAPRIKA
1/8 tsp. BLACK PEPPER
4 oz. HEAVY CREAM
1/4 cup GREEN ONIONS, diced
2 1/2 Tbsp. BUTTER, soft
SALT, to taste
1 LEMON, cut into quarters, then sliced to make fan
4 BELL PEPPERS, cut in half and seeded

In a large skillet, sauté shrimp in olive oil, add garlic and mushrooms. Deglaze pan with white wine and reduce. Add seasonings and cream, reduce. Add onions, simmer, remove from heat and fold in butter slowly. Salt to taste. Broil pepper bottoms and distribute the shrimp between them. Pour sauce over shrimp, garnish with lemon fan and a sprig of dill.

> *Set high above the Methow Valley, which is home to ten times more deer than people, Sun Mountain Lodge offers rustic elegance and Four Diamond Award-winning dining in the heart of the North Cascade mountains. In the nearby historic western theme town of Winthrop, visitors may even encounter a cattle drive down the main street!*

Breakfasts

Swedish Pancakes

U. S. Senator Patty Murray — Washington, D. C.

1 1/2 cups FLOUR
1 scant tsp. SALT
3 tsp. SUGAR
3 large EGGS or 4 smaller EGGS
2 cups MILK
1 Tbsp. BUTTER, melted

Combine the flour, salt and sugar in a bowl. Whip the eggs and milk together, then blend slowly into the dry mixture, and add the melted butter. For one large pancake, pour the batter into a greased 12 inch cast iron skillet and bake in a pre-heated 350 degree oven until brown. Serve sprinkled with lemon juice, powdered sugar and fresh fruit such as strawberries. For individual pancakes, use a scant half cup of batter per pancake and fry in a greased skillet. These will be very thin and can be rolled. They can also be sprinkled with lemon juice, and powdered sugar and served with fresh fruit.

White Salmon Maple Treats

The Inn of the White Salmon — White Salmon

Sauce:
   3/4 cup MAPLE SYRUP
   1/2 cup BUTTER (1 cube)
   3/4 cup BROWN SUGAR, lightly packed
   1/2 cup chopped WALNUTS

Filling:
   1 (8 oz. pkg.) CREAM CHEESE, at room temperature
   3 Tbsp. BUTTER
   1/4 cup POWDERED SUGAR
   1/2 cup COCONUT, shredded and sweetened

Buttermilk biscuit dough:
   NOTE: To make dough, follow your favorite recipe. If you're in a hurry, use ready-to-bake biscuits. Varieties 10 to a package can be split in half to equal 20.

Prepare sauce in a small saucepan, by combining maple syrup and butter. Cook over low heat until butter is melted. Stir in brown sugar until it is dissolved and well-blended. Add walnuts. Divide mixture between two 9-inch pie plates.

Prepare filling in a mixing bowl with an electric mixer, by creaming together cream cheese and butter. Sift powdered sugar into cream cheese mixture and blend with a wooden spoon; stir in coconut.

Roll out the prepared biscuit dough to 1/4 inch thickness. Cut 20 3-inch-round biscuits. Flatten each circle with your hand to form a 4-inch round. Place 1 tsp. of filling in center and wrap dough around it, pinching edges to seal in filling. (Leftover filling will keep refrigerated for up to a week.) Set each biscuit in the pie pan, 10 per pie pan. Bake for 20 minutes or until biscuits are light brown. Serve warm. Makes 10 servings.

The Inn of the White Salmon was built in 1937, not far from the banks of the mighty Columbia River. Here, you may sample fresh-baked breads, tarts, pastries and egg dishes.

Saucy Eggs

4 Tbsp. BUTTER
4 Tbsp. FLOUR
1/2 tsp. GARLIC SALT
1/2 tsp. SALT
1/4 tsp. PEPPER
1 tsp. WORCESTERSHIRE SAUCE
1 1/2 cups MILK
1/4 lb. GRATED CHEDDAR CHEESE
6 EGGS
3 ENGLISH MUFFINS, split and toasted

In heavy saucepan, melt butter and slowly add flour, stirring to make a smooth paste. Add seasonings, Worcestershire and milk, stirring rapidly to keep smooth. Cook until thickened, and blend in the grated cheese. Pour half the mixture into greased 10 x 6 baking dish. Break egg into small cup and carefully pour atop the cheese. Do this with all 6 eggs. Pour remainder of sauce around eggs. Bake at 350 degrees for about 20 minutes, until eggs are set. To serve, place one egg and cheese sauce atop toasted muffin half. Serve with sausage links, Canadian bacon or ham.

The Shelburne Inn is on Washington's Long Beach Peninsula, an unspoiled 28-mile stretch of wild Pacific sea coast known as the longest, continuous beach in the United States. Operated by David Campiche and Laurie Anderson, this inn has been a landmark in Seaview since its opening in 1896.

Salmon Potato Cakes

The Shelburne Inn — Seaview

1/2 YELLOW ONION, chopped
1 1/2 Tbsp. BUTTER
4 large POTATOES, peeled, cooked, drained and mashed
2 1/2 lb. SALMON FILLET, baked, skin and bones removed
1/3 cup HEAVY CREAM
3 Tbsp. melted BUTTER
1/4 tsp. MACE
1/4 tsp. NUTMEG
3/4 tsp. SALT
1/2 tsp. freshly ground BLACK PEPPER
1 EGG
2 Tbsp. fresh DILL, chopped
1 1/2 cup fresh BREAD CRUMBS, seasoned with SALT, freshly
   ground BLACK PEPPER, PAPRIKA and CAYENNE PEPPER
   to taste
BUTTER for reheating

Sauté onion in butter until tender; add to mashed potatoes. Next, add the salmon, cream, butter, mace, nutmeg, salt, black pepper, egg and dill. Mix these ingredients together. Now prepare the bread crumb mixture. Form 4 inch wide patties by hand and dip each side into the seasoned bread crumbs and refrigerate until ready for use. Melt a little butter over medium heat in a sauté pan and place patties in it until heated through, turning once. Serve with a poached egg and *Hollandaise Sauce.*

Hollandaise Sauce

6 EGG YOLKS
2 Tbsp. fresh-squeezed LEMON JUICE
1/2 lb. unsalted BUTTER, melted
1/2 tsp. SALT
1/8 tsp. CAYENNE PEPPER

Put egg yolks and lemon juice in a 2-quart stainless steel bowl. Place over very hot, but not boiling water, making sure the bowl does not touch the water. Whip with a wire whisk until the yolks are the consistency of heavy cream. Very slowly, whisk in the melted butter until the sauce thickens even more. As you add more butter (at first, in minute quantities) and the sauce thickens, you can begin to add it a little faster. Finally, add the salt and cayenne pepper.

'37 House Benedict

'37 House Bed and Breakfast — Yakima

4 ENGLISH MUFFINS, split, toasted and buttered
8 slices ripe TOMATO
12 slices BACON, cooked and crumbled
8 poached EGGS
PAPRIKA

Dip the tomato slices in flour and fry in bacon fat. Place a tomato slice on each half of muffin, and add crumbled bacon. Top with egg, and cover with 2 cups of *Blender Hollandaise,* a few more small pieces of bacon and a sprinkle of paprika.

Blender Hollandaise

3 EGG YOLKS
2 Tbsp. LEMON JUICE, fresh squeezed
1 dash CAYENNE PEPPER
1 dash WHITE PEPPER
1/2 cup BUTTER, boiling
SALT to taste

Place first four ingredients in blender, and blend for a couple seconds. Add boiling butter gradually to blended ingredients until all is used. Blend a few more seconds. If the sauce is too thin, the butter was not hot enough. Heat the whole mixture in the microwave until thickened. Serves 4.

> *Pasco, Richland and Kennewick, nearby, are located at the confluence of the Snake, Yakima and Columbia Rivers, and are known as the "Tri-Cities", enjoying nearly 300 days of sunshine each year. The Columbia is the 2nd largest river in North America.*

Buttermilk Pancakes

Jerry Walker, Bellingham Giants — Bellingham

2 cups FLOUR, sifted
1 tsp. SALT
1 1/4 tsp. SODA
3/4 tsp. BAKING POWDER
2 EGGS
2 cups DARIGOLD® BUTTERMILK
1/4 cup OIL
CHOCOLATE CHIPS, if desired

Sift dry ingredients together. Combine liquid ingredients and stir lightly into flour mixture. Batter will be lumpy. Spoon onto greased griddle and while baking, sprinkle with chocolate chips. Turn when bubbles appear. Try adding M & M's® for a different taste treat. Serves 4.

"A family favorite for over forty years. I find the secret to this recipe is the use of Washington's own Darigold Buttermilk."

> *Bellingham, located just 24 miles from the Canadian Border, is the southern terminus for the Alaska Ferry. It is also the home of the Bellingham Giants, the Class A affiliate of the San Francisco Giants.*

Heavenly, Crab-Filled Croissants

Albatross Bed & Breakfast — Anacortes

4 lg. CROISSANTS
8 EGGS
3 Tbsp. MILK
1 Tbsp. PARSLEY, minced, fresh
1/3 cup MUSHROOMS, chopped
1/2 cup FRESH CRAB, chopped
4 Tbsp. BUTTER
1/4 cup SWISS CHEESE, shredded
1/4 cup CHEDDAR CHEESE, shredded

Warm croissants in oven 5 minutes before filling. In a bowl, beat eggs and milk together. Add parsley, mushrooms and crab. Melt butter in skillet. Pour egg mixture into skillet, cooking and stirring over low heat until creamy. Preheat broiler. Slice croissants, leaving attached. Fill bottom half with egg mixture and sprinkle both sides with cheese. Broil open-face until the cheese is melted. Serve immediately. Serves 4.

In Anacortes, between 1924 and 1943, the E. K. Wood Mill Company operated one of the largest and finest lumber mills in the state. The author's father was among the mill workers. As the lumber activity waned, giving way to today's firmly based tourist industry, the lumber mill was dismantled. The only two remaining structures are the planing mill and the mill manager's home that was constructed in 1927. This home is now open to the public and is known as the Albatross. It is a lovely Cape Cod-style home, with a large view deck.

Banana Pecan Pancakes

The Shelburne Inn — Seaview

2 BANANAS
2 EGGS
3 cups BUTTERMILK
3 Tbsp. BUTTER, melted
2 cups UNBLEACHED
    WHITE FLOUR
1 tsp. BAKING SODA

1/2 tsp. SALT
1 cup CORNMEAL
1/2 cup BRAN
1 Tbsp. HONEY
1/2 cup PECANS
    (sautéed in butter)

In a medium bowl, mash the bananas with a fork until the lumps are mostly worked out. Then add the eggs, buttermilk and melted butter. Mix thoroughly. In a separate bowl, sift the flour with the baking soda and salt, then stir in the bran and cornmeal. Now add the dry ingredients to the banana mixture, stirring until the dry ingredients are moistened. Finally, add the nuts and honey and you're ready to prepare them just as you do any other pancakes. Heat a griddle to 350 degrees, spoon on the batter and cook the pancakes until they're golden brown on both sides.

*"We accompany these pancakes with either maple syrup or our own homemade **Cranberry Orange Sauce**."*

Cranberry Orange Sauce

24 oz. fresh CRANBERRIES
1 1/2 cup WATER
2 cups SUGAR
1/2 cup DRY WHITE WINE

1 ORANGE (juice and
    grated rind)
1 stick CINNAMON

Add the sugar to the water and bring to a boil, then add the cranberries and remaining ingredients. Bring it to a boil, then lower heat and for 15-20 minutes. Remove the cinnamon stick and strain the mixture, reserving the liquid. Place the ingredients from the sieve into a food processor and process for one minute. Pour this mixture and the reserved liquid into a saucepan along with the cinnamon stick and simmer for 15 more minutes to thicken. Serve warm over pancakes.

Apple Oatcakes

Campbell's Resort — Chelan

1 1/2 cup WHEAT FLOUR
1 1/4 cup WHITE FLOUR
1 cup GROUND OATMEAL
1 Tbsp. BAKING POWDER
4 tsp. BAKING SODA
1 tsp. SALT

1/4 lb. BUTTER
1 cup EGGS
1 qt. BUTTERMILK
1/2 cup HONEY
1/4 YELLOW APPLE, diced

Mix first 6 ingredients, and cut in butter in a food processor or with pastry cutter, then add eggs, buttermilk and honey. Sprinkle apples on oatcake before flipping over on grill. These take a little longer than a regular hotcake and tend to be a little darker. Blueberries or raisins may be substituted for apples, if you wish.

Groveland Hot Cereal

Simone's Groveland Cottage Bed & Breakfast — Sequim

4 cups WATER
2 cups MIXED GRAINS
1 Tbsp. CINNAMON
1/4 tsp. SALT
1 APPLE, grated

1/4 cup GOLDEN RAISINS
1/4 cup DARK RAISINS
1/4 cup CURRANTS
1/2 cup WALNUTS, chopped

Combine in a large container equal parts of rolled: Thick Oats, Triticale, Rye, Barley and Red Wheat. Boil the water and add cinnamon, salt, grains, apple, raisins and currants. Mix well and then add the walnuts, but do not stir in, just place on top. Turn heat to low and steam for 30 minutes. Serve in bowls, offering brown sugar, milk, cream or plain yogurt. When in season, we also use fresh berries to top off the cereal. If you are on a low-fat diet, simply leave out the nuts, and use skim milk or non-fat yogurt. Delicious. Serves 6.

Much of the original decor has been retained at the turn of the century Groveland Cottage Bed and Breakfast. The Great Room of the inn, with its massive river rock fireplace, has been turned into a country store.

Smoked Salmon & Creme Fraiche Omelette

The Twickenham House Bed & Breakfast — Langley

1/2 RED ONION, sliced thinly
OLIVE OIL, as needed
2 cups CILANTRO, fresh, chopped
1/4 lb. SMOKED SALMON
SALT and PEPPER to taste
3 EGGS
CREME FRAICHE

Quickly sauté onion in olive oil, then add the cilantro and a dash of black ground pepper. Add smoked salmon and heat through; be sure not to over cook the salmon. Keep warm in covered dish in oven. To make omelette, whip eggs, salt and pepper. Heat olive oil in sauté pan, and add egg mixture. When omelette is barely golden on one side, add salmon/cilantro mixture, and a dollop of creme fraiche, then fold. Serve immediately on hot plate. Garnish with a drizzle of *Lemon-Chive Creme Fraiche* and sprinkle with very fine chopped parsley.

Lemon-Chive Creme Fraiche

2 cups SOUR CREAM
1/2 cup BUTTERMILK
1/2 cup WHIPPING CREAM
1 tsp. LEMON JUICE, fresh
1 tsp. DIJON MUSTARD
FRESH CRACKED PEPPER to taste
1 Tbsp. CHIVES, fresh, chopped

Mix all ingredients together in a large bowl. Refrigerate until ready to use. It will keep for days if refrigerated.

Clafouti

(a French Flan)

Moon and Sixpence Bed & Breakfast — Friday Harbor

1 1/4 cup 2% MILK
1/3 cup SUGAR
3 EGGS
2 tsp. VANILLA EXTRACT
2/3 cup FLOUR
1 1/2 cups BING CHERRIES, pitted
1/3 cup SUGAR
POWDERED SUGAR for sprinkling

Place greased pie pan on stove top burner set at medium heat. In a processor, mix the milk, sugar, eggs and vanilla, and beat 1 minute. Add half the flour and blend 30 seconds. Add remaining flour and blend another 30 seconds. Pour 1/4 inch of batter into heated pie pan. Keep pan on the burner for two minutes or until a film of batter has set on bottom of pan. Remove from heat and spread cherries over the batter. Sprinkle with the other 1/3 cup sugar. Pour rest of batter over cherries, and bake at 350 degrees for one hour. Cool a few minutes and then cut into 6 pie shaped servings. Sprinkle with powdered sugar and serve on breakfast plate with a light meat such as thin-sliced, cold, smoked turkey.

Moon and Sixpence is a classic country bed and breakfast in the incomparable San Juan Islands. This remodeled dairy farm was built in the early 1900's. The cattle are gone, but sheep graze lazily in the nearby pasture. Charles and Evelyn Tuller own and operate the inn. Evelyn also operates a weaving studio on the grounds. Together, they founded the society that maintains an island museum of spinning and weaving equipment where the colors of the San Juans become glowingly visible on restored looms.

Ricotta Pancakes

Turtleback Farm Inn — Orcas Island

3 EGGS, separated
1 cup RICOTTA CHEESE
2/3 cup MILK
1/4 cup WHITE FLOUR

1/4 cup WHOLE WHEAT
  FLOUR
1 tsp. BAKING POWDER
1 pinch SALT

Beat egg whites until stiff, but not dry. To the yolks, add remaining ingredients, blending until thoroughly mixed. Fold the whites into the batter. Bake on a greased, hot griddle until golden brown. Serve with butter and syrup or honey.

Six miles up Old Crow Road from the ferry landing is a sign announcing your arrival at Turtleback Farm Inn, so named by owners Bill and Susan Fletcher after the turtle-shaped mountain nearby. Susan, daughter of the late actor Buster Crabbe, has filled the inn with braided rugs on polished hardwood floors and antiques rich with regional memories. The inn has been chosen by the Los Angeles Times as one of the dozen most romantic spots in the U.S. ♥ ♥ ♥

Spiced Waffles

Turtleback Farm Inn — Orcas Island

1 cup WHOLE WHEAT FLOUR
3/4 cup WHITE FLOUR
1/4 cup ROLLED OATS or
    OAT FLOUR
2 tsp. BAKING POWDER
1 tsp. SODA
1/2 tsp. SALT

1 Tbsp. SUGAR
1/2 tsp. CINNAMON
1/4 tsp. NUTMEG
1/2 tsp. ALLSPICE
2 cups BUTTERMILK
6 Tbsp. BUTTER, melted, cooled
2 EGGS, separated

Sift dry ingredients, then blend into buttermilk, which you have already blended with the butter and yolks. Fold in beaten whites, (beaten stiff but not dry), until just blended. Bake on waffle iron, serving with butter and honey blended together in equal amounts, to which a little orange zest has been added.

Downey House Granola

Downey House Bed & Breakfast — La Conner

4 cups OLD FASHIONED OATS, not instant or quick
2/3 cup WHEAT GERM
2/3 cup UNSWEETENED BIG FLAKE COCONUT
6 Tbsp. SESAME SEEDS
6 Tbsp. SUNFLOWER SEEDS
1/2 cup RAW CASHEWS, in pieces (or sliced almonds)
2/3 cup CORN OIL
1/3 cup HONEY
1 tsp. VANILLA
1/4 tsp. SALT
1/2 cup DRIED FRUIT (or raisins)

Mix first six ingredients in large bowl. In a saucepan, combine corn oil, honey, vanilla, and salt. Cook over low heat until honey is melted. Pour over dry mixture and blend thoroughly. Spread on lightly greased pan and bake at 300 degrees for 35 to 45 minutes, stirring every 10 minutes. Cool and add fruit, if desired. Homemade granola is easy to make, and is so handy to have stored in the freezer in ziplock bags for ready use. Serve plain with milk, over yogurt, or over hot applesauce. Add whipped cream to the applesauce and granola for a tasty dessert.

Locals swarm to the historic waterfront town of La Conner every year to jig smelt. La Conner, located on the Swinomish Channel, is where tourists flock by the thousands to browse in delightful arts-and-crafts shops.

Soups & Chowders

Ocean Crest Original Clam Chowder

Ocean Crest Dinner House — Moclips

2 cups WATER
1 lg. POTATO, diced
1/3 cup ONION, diced
1/3 cup CELERY, diced
2 slices BACON
1/2 tsp. SALT

1/2 cup CLAMS, chopped, well drained
1 can CONDENSED MILK
1 tsp. BUTTER
PARSLEY or CHIVES, chopped

Cook first six ingredients together just until tender. Add clams. Heat and add milk. Do not boil. Place butter and parsley/chives in each individual serving bowl, and pour hot chowder over this. Serve at once.

This family-operated resort, perched high on a bluff overlooking the Pacific Ocean, features fresh seafood and Northwest regional cuisine. Over 40 years ago when there were only 4 tables, reservations were required. Today, they still serve the same chowder and have 3 dining rooms. Reservations are "advised".

Award-Winning Clam Chowder

Arnie's Restaurants — Mukilteo, Edmonds and Seattle

5 lbs. RED POTATOES, 1/2 in. cubes
3 cans (46 oz. ea.) CLAM JUICE
1 1/2 lb. ONION, diced
1 lb. CELERY, diced
1/3 lb. CARROT, grated
3 oz. GARLIC, minced
1/2 Tbsp. THYME, dried whole
4 BAY LEAVES
2 cups WHITE WINE
8 1/2 oz. CLAM BASE (Clam soup paste) (2 Tbsp. SALT can be substituted)
1 can (28 oz.) BABY CLAMS
1 Tbsp. BLACK PEPPER
1/2 Tbsp. NUTMEG
3 qt. WHIPPING CREAM
2 cups PANKO® JAPANESE-STYLE BREAD CRUMBS
1/2 cup BACON, diced, cooked
1/2 cup PARSLEY, chopped, fresh
1/2 cup FLOUR and 1/2 cup VEGETABLE OIL mixed together for roux

In heavy bottom pan, simmer diced potatoes in clam juice 15-20 minutes until slightly crisp. Add diced onions, celery, carrots, garlic, thyme, bay leaves, white wine and clam base and simmer 15-20 minutes until potatoes are soft, but not mushy. The onions, celery and carrots should be slightly crisp. Add clams, pepper, nutmeg and cream and bring back to slow boil. Add panko, bacon, parsley and roux. Simmer 10-15 more minutes. Yield about 3 gallons.

Apple, Potato & Cheddar Soup

Washington Apple Commission

2 Tbsp. VEGETABLE OIL
3 medium GRANNY SMITH APPLES, peeled, cored, chopped
1 POTATO, peeled, chopped
1 stalk CELERY, chopped
1/4 cup ONION, finely chopped
1/8 tsp. GROUND THYME
1/4 cup WHITE WINE
5 cups CHICKEN STOCK
4 cups MILD CHEDDAR CHEESE, grated
1/2 cup HEAVY CREAM
1/8 tsp. NUTMEG
SALT and WHITE PEPPER
BUTTERED CROUTONS
APPLES, peeled, diced

Heat oil in large sauce pot; add apples, potato, celery, onion and thyme. Sauté 10 minutes, then stir in wine and simmer 2 minutes. Add stock and simmer 45 minutes. Purée soup mixture. Return to sauce pot. Over very low heat, stir in cheese, cream, nutmeg, salt and pepper to taste. Cook just till heated through (do not boil). Garnish with croutons and diced apples. Serves 4.

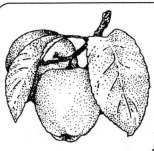

Were you aware that Delicious apples were originally called Hawkeyes? They were renamed after a state fair judge bit into one and remarked "Delicious!" Stark Brothers nurseries sent samples of Delicious trees in all its orders, and soon, 8 million trees were planted. The original tree died in 1940, a victim of sub-zero frost. The Apple Commision in Wenatchee features informative apple-related displays, recipes, souvenirs, video presentation and an inviting glass of apple juice.

Creamy Tomato-Mushroom Soup

Former Congressman Al Swift, U. S. House of Representatives

1 1/2 TOMATOES, peeled, seeded, saving juice
2 cubes CHICKEN BOUILLON
1 cup ONIONS, diced
1 lg. CELERY RIB, diced
1 lg. clove GARLIC, minced
1/2 lb. MUSHROOMS, diced
BUTTER

1 1/2 tsp. CUMIN
1 tsp. TARRAGON (or BASIL)
1 tsp. BOUQUET GARNIE®
1 1/2 cups CREAM, HALF & HALF, or MILK
TOMATO or V8® JUICE
6 drops TABASCO®, optional

Prepare tomatoes and dissolve the chicken bouillon in the juice. Sauté the onion, celery, garlic and mushrooms. When soft, add tomatoes and their juice mixed with bouillon. Simmer with all the spices, adjusting flavor as you go. When cooked, blend in a food processor until smooth. (If you prefer, leave some chunks.) Return to heat, adjust seasonings as required, and add cream, and tomato juice to achieve desired consistency. Serve piping hot with croutons, a dollop of sour cream, a sprinkle of chives or other garnish.

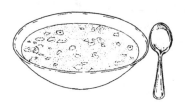

Cream of Cheese Soup

3 cups POTATOES, cubed
1 cup WATER
1/2 cup CELERY, sliced
1/2 cup CARROT, sliced
1/4 cup ONION, chopped
1 tsp. PARSLEY FLAKES
1/2 tsp. SALT

1/2 tsp. PEPPER
1 CHICKEN BOUILLION CUBE
1 1/2 cups MILK
2 Tbsp. FLOUR
1/2 lb. PROCESSED CHEESE, cubed

Combine first 8 ingredients in Dutch oven, cover and simmer until tender. Combine milk with flour, stir into soup. Add cheese and stir until melted.

Old Fashioned Cream of Tomato Soup

4B's Restaurants

32 oz. TOMATOES, canned, diced
9 oz. CHICKEN BROTH, undiluted
1 oz. BUTTER
2 Tbsp. SUGAR
1 Tbsp. ONION, chopped
2 cups CREAM
1 pinch BAKING SODA

Mix tomatoes, chicken broth, butter, sugar, onion and soda and simmer 1 hour. Heat cream in double boiler. Add cream to hot tomato mixture and serve. Yields 1/2 gallon.

Tomatoes are widely grown in the lower Yakima Valley, along with many varieties of fruit. This is also the state's prime wine region, with more than a dozen wineries. Long before the Lewis & Clark expedition came through the valley in 1805, Indian tribes hunted, fished and farmed the rich farm lands. It is one of the nation's leading producers of hops. The world's single largest hop field (1,836 acres) is in Toppenish.

Oyster Stew

1/4 CUP BUTTER
1 pt. OYSTERS, with liquor
3/4 tsp. SALT
2 cups MILK

1/2 cup HALF & HALF
dash PEPPER
dash HOT PEPPER SAUCE
PAPRIKA

In sauce pan, melt butter, adding oysters with their liquor. Cook gently until edges of oysters begin to curl. Meanwhile, heat the milk and half & half to scalding point. Add oysters and seasonings to taste. Sprinkle with paprika and serve immediately.

Owned by the Coast Oyster Company, the world's largest oyster hatchery is in Quilcene.

Northwest Shrimp Soup

3 med. ONIONS, sliced
1/4 cup MARGARINE
1 cup BOILING WATER
4 med. POTATOES, diced
SALT, PEPPER to taste
1 1/2 qts. MILK
3 cups GRATED CHEESE
2 lbs. SHRIMP, fresh, peeled
3 Tbsp. FRESH PARSLEY, chopped

Sauté onions in margarine; add boiling water, then diced potatoes and salt and pepper. Simmer until potatoes are tender. Combine milk and cheese and heat together until cheese melts. Do not boil. Set aside. Add shrimp to potatoes and cook until the shrimp is pink, about 3 minutes. Remove from stove and add milk and cheese mixture. Sprinkle with parsley.

'Specially Good Potato Soup

3 Tbsp. MARGARINE
1 med. CARROT, diced
1/4 cup ONION, diced
2 Tbsp. FLOUR
1 qt. MILK
1 CHICKEN BOUILLON CUBE
6 med. POTATOES, cooked,
    diced
2 Tbsp. PARSLEY
1 tsp. SALT
1/2 tsp. SEASONING SALT
PEPPER to taste

Melt margarine in large pan, add carrot and onion. Cook until tender. Blend in flour and gradually stir in milk and bouillon cube. When slightly thick, add half the potatoes and stir in the parsley and the seasonings. Mash remaining potatoes and stir into the soup. Serves 4.

Tropical Apple Salad Platter

Mike Lowry, Governor - State of Washington — Olympia

1 GOLDEN DELICIOUS WASHINGTON APPLE
1 RED DELICIOUS WASHINGTON APPLE
1 PINEAPPLE, fresh, cored and cut into spears
1 HONEYDEW MELON, pared and cut into chunks
1 PAPAYA, pared and sliced
1 BANANA, peeled and sliced
2 ctns. (6-8 oz. ea.) LOW-FAT LEMON YOGURT
2 Tbsp. HONEY
2 Tbsp. LIME JUICE

Core and slice apples, and arrange fruits on a large platter. Make ***Lime Cream Dressing*** by combining yogurt, honey and lime juice in a small bowl. Stir just enough to mix well. Serves 8.

The old capitol building, originally the Thurston County Courthouse, is located in central Olympia. The state legislature first met here in March, 1904.

Canlis Special Salad

Canlis Restaurant — Seattle

Salad:
> **1 to 2 TOMATOES, peeled, ripe**
> **1 lg. head ROMAINE LETTUCE (Wash individual leaves in warm water, drain and dry in colander, chill in refrigerator)**

Condiments:
> **1/2 cup chopped GREEN ONION**
> **3/4 cup freshly grated ROMANO CHEESE**
> **1/2 cup BACON, very well done, chopped**
> **1/2 tsp. OREGANO**
> **4 Tbsp. chopped fresh MINT (can't use too much)**
> **1/2 tsp. SALT**
> **1/2 cup CROUTONS, garlic flavored preferred**

Dressing:
> **1 LEMON, juiced**
> **1 tsp. FRESH GROUND PEPPER**
> **1 CODDLED EGG**
> **1/2 cup OLIVE OIL (flavored with garlic cloves)**

Into a large bowl, place the tomatoes, cut into eighths. Add cold lettuce, sliced into one-inch squares. Then add green onions, cheese (save some to sprinkle on top), bacon, oregano and 1/2 of the mint. To make dressing, put lemon juice, pepper, egg and balance of mint in a bowl and whip vigorously. Then slowly add olive oil, whipping constantly. Pour over salad, toss thoroughly. Add croutons, and a sprinkle of Romano last.

Sightseeing boats depart from Seattle's waterfront, with cruises across Puget Sound to Tillicum Village. Here you can be treated to an Indian salmon bake, and costumed tribal dances in an authentic cedar "longhouse".

Favorite Cranberry Salad

Jerry and Lisa Walker — Bellingham

1 lb. GROUND CRANBERRIES	1 lb. MARSHMALLOWS,
1 cup SUGAR	cut into quarters
1 can (20 oz.) CRUSHED PINEAPPLE	1 pt. WHIPPING CREAM

Mix cranberries and sugar together, and let sit overnight. Combine crushed pineapple and marshmallows together, and let them sit overnight separately. The next day, combine the mixtures, mixing well. Whip the cream, and combine. If you freeze the cranberries, they will grind with very little mess. You need to be sure you have 16 oz. of cranberries and marshmallows, not just the 12 oz. package. This is an exceptional salad for Christmas and Thanksgiving.

> *Cranberries are grown on the Long Beach peninsula in the southwestern corner of Washington—known as the Cranberry Coast. In the fall, right before the harvest, the fields near Seaview become bright red carpets on the landscape. Grayland has a cranberry museum.*

Cranberry Molded Salad

1 pkg. (6 oz.) STRAWBERRY GELATIN
2 cups WATER, boiling
1 tsp. ORANGE RIND, grated
1 can (20 oz.) CRUSHED PINEAPPLE, drained, save juice
2 Tbsp. LEMON JUICE
1 cup FRESH CRANBERRIES, chopped
1/2 cup CELERY, diced
2/3 cup WALNUTS, chopped

Dissolve gelatin in water. Stir in orange rind. Pour reserved pineapple juice into 2 cup measure. Add lemon juice and enough cold water to total 2 cups. Stir into gelatin mixture.

Refrigerate 60-90 minutes until consistency of unbeaten egg white. Fold in cranberries, celery, walnuts and pineapple. Pour into lightly oiled 2 quart mold. Chill at least 24 hours. Line round platter with lettuce leaves. Loosen edge of mold with thin knife. Dip mold quickly in hot water to loosen. Invert on to lettuce. Serves 12.

Music Salad

1 sm. pkg. LEMON GELATIN
1 cup HOT WATER
1 cup MAYONNAISE
1 sm. can SHRIMP, drained
1 can (8 1/4 oz.) CRUSHED PINEAPPLE, drained
3 sm. CARROTS, grated
1 glass PIMIENTO CHEESE

Dissolve gelatin in hot water. Combine with other ingredients and place in 10 x 7 glass dish and refrigerate.

Seafood Pasta Salad

1/2 cup SALAD DRESSING
1/4 cup ZESTY ITALIAN DRESSING
2 cups (8 oz.) CORKSCREW NOODLES,
    cooked and drained
1 1/2 cups CRAB MEAT
1 cup TOMATOES, chopped
1 cup BROCCOLI FLOWERETTES,
    partially cooked
1/2 cup GREEN PEPPER, chopped
1/4 cup GREEN ONION, sliced

Combine dressings, and mix well. Add remaining ingredients, and mix lightly. Chill. Serves 4.

Asparagus Salad Romana

American Fine Foods, canners of Walla Walla® vegetables.

1/2 cup MAYONNAISE
1/4 cup ITALIAN STYLE DRESSING
1 can (15 oz.) ASPARAGUS SPEARS,
    chilled, drained
1 tsp. PAPRIKA
ROMAINE LETTUCE

Blend mayonnaise with dressing. Spoon over asparagus spears arranged on Romaine leaf lettuce. Sprinkle with paprika. Serves 4.

San Francisco Salad

Melva Hillhouse — Everett

1 pkg. CHICKEN FLAVORED RICE-A-RONI®
1 jar (6 oz.) MARINATED ARTICHOKE HEARTS
1 can (4 1/2 oz.) BLACK OLIVES, chopped
2 GREEN ONIONS, finely chopped
1/2 cup MAYONNAISE
1/2 tsp. CURRY POWDER

Prepare rice according to directions. Drain artichokes, saving liquid, and chop. While rice is still warm, add artichokes, olives and green onions. Combine mayonnaise, artichoke liquid and curry powder; blending well. Stir into rice mixture. Serve immediately or chill. Serves 4.

The world's largest building, by volume, is located in Everett. Here, the Boeing Company assembles the massive 747, 767 and 777 widebody aircraft. There are six million parts in the 747. The wing area of a 747-400 is large enough to hold 45 medium-sized automobiles. More than 1.4 billion passengers have travelled more than 17.9 billion miles since 1970 in a 747 jet, which is as tall as a six-story building. This 1,000-acre site employs more than 25,000 people, has enough floor space to accommodate 57 football fields or 568 basketball courts.

Hot Chicken Salad

Laura Kain — Everett

2 cups CHICKEN, cooked, diced
1 can CREAM OF CHICKEN SOUP
1 3/4 cup INSTANT RICE, cooked
3/4 cup MAYONNAISE
1/4 cup WATER
3 tsp. LEMON JUICE
1 cup ALMOND, slivered
1 cup CELERY, diced
3 EGGS, hard cooked, mashed
2 tsp. ONION, diced
1/2 tsp. SALT

Combine all ingredients in large mixing bowl and mix well. Place in a buttered casserole, top with crushed corn flakes or bread crumbs about 1/4 inch thick. Bake in 350 degree oven about 30 minutes.

Golden Pepper Pasta Salad

Washington Apple Commission — Wenatchee

1 GOLDEN DELICIOUS APPLE, cored, diced
1 1/2 cups cooked PASTA
1 cup RED, GREEN or YELLOW PEPPER, thinly sliced
1/2 cup CHEDDAR CHEESE, shredded
SALT and PEPPER

Prepare *Vinaigrette Dressing* (below) and set aside. In a large bowl, combine apple, pasta, peppers and cheese. Pour dressing over all, and toss to blend. Season to taste and serve.

Vinaigrette Dressing

2 Tbsp. WHITE WINE VINEGAR
2 Tbsp. VEGETABLE OIL
1/2 tsp. OREGANO, dried
1/2 tsp. THYME, dried
1/2 tsp. LEMON PEEL, grated

In small bowl, combine all together and mix well. — "Pasta is a wonderful medium for combining flavors and textures. In this fool-proof dish, apple meets pepper and cheese."

In addition to tasting super-delicious, Washington apples are a virtual fiber factory. Fiber (apple pectin) helps to lower your blood cholesterol. Apples have less sodium than ordinary tap water and no cholesterol. They contain niacin, calcium, iron, potassium, phosphorous, vitamins A, B, B2 and C, and boron to help prevent osteoporosis.

Crab or Shrimp Dressing

Jimmie Holeman — Everett

1 cup CRAB MEAT, or SHRIMP, drained
1 Tbsp. LEMON JUICE
3 GREEN ONIONS, chopped
1 cup SOUR CREAM
1/4 cup MAYONNAISE
1/4 tsp. SALT
1/8 tsp. PEPPER
1/8 tsp. GARLIC SALT
1/8 tsp. TARRAGON
LETTUCE

Combine all ingredients and spoon over wedges of lettuce. Serves 4.

Two-Apple Waldorf Salad

The Apple Growers of Washington State

2 RED DELICIOUS APPLES, cored, cubed
2 GRANNY SMITH APPLES, cored, cubed
2 Tbsp. ORANGE JUICE
1 cup CELERY, sliced
1 cup WALNUTS, broken
2 Tbsp. CURRANTS (or raisins)
HONEY-YOGURT DRESSING

Combine apples with orange juice. Add celery, walnuts, currants and *Honey-Yogurt Dressing* or *Waldorf Salad Dressing.* Mix thoroughly. Serves 6-8.

Honey-Yogurt Dressing

2/3 cup PLAIN YOGURT
1/3 cup MAYONNAISE
1 Tbsp. ORANGE PEEL, grated
1 Tbsp. HONEY

Mix all ingredients. Chill at least 1 hour. Makes 1 cup.

Waldorf Salad Dressing

In small bowl, whisk together:

1/3 cup OIL
3 Tbsp. each RED WINE VINEGAR and thawed frozen APPLE
    JUICE CONCENTRATE
3/4 tsp. DILL WEED
SALT and PEPPER to taste

Stir in:
1 cup BLUE CHEESE or FETA CHEESE, crumbled

> *As you travel through central Washington, you will see more than 4,000 apple orchards scattered from Maryhill to Tonasket. More than 45,000 pickers are needed for the six-week harvest, about half of which are year-round residents. Many of the apples are shipped from the largest cold storage facility on the West Coast at the Port of Seattle (The Emerald City), which ships 3 million boxes annually.*

Tuna Salad

3/4 cup MAYONNAISE
1/2 cup SOUR CREAM
1/4 cup CUCUMBER, chopped
2 Tbsp. ONION, chopped
2 EGGS, hard cooked
1/2 tsp. DILL WEED
1 1/2 qts. assorted GREENS, torn
2 cans (6-1/2 oz. ea.) TUNA, drained, flaked
TOMATO WEDGES

Separate the egg, using the white in the salad, and the yolk for garnish. Mix salad dressing, sour cream, cucumber, onion, chopped egg whites, and dill weed. Chill. For each serving, top greens with tuna and dressing. Garnish with sieved egg yolk and wedged tomatoes. Serves 4.

Taco Macaroni Salad

Joyce Fowler — Puyallup

1 pkg. (7 oz.) MACARONI
1 pkg. (12 oz.) GROUND
  SAUSAGE
1 can KIDNEY BEANS, drained
1 can (8 oz.) WHOLE KERNEL
  CORN, drained
2 TOMATOES, diced
1 GREEN PEPPER, diced

1/4 cup ONIONS, diced
1/2 cup RIPE OLIVES, sliced
1 cup CHEESE, grated
1/2 cup TACO SAUCE
1/4 cup SALAD OIL
1 tsp. SEASONING SALT
1 tsp. SWEET BASIL LEAVES

Cook macaroni and drain. Fry sausage and drain. Combine sausage, beans, corn, tomatoes, peppers, onions, olives and cheese. In another bowl, blend together taco sauce, oil, salt and basil. Combine with sausage mixture adding cooked macaroni. Toss all together and chill. Serves 6-8.

The Puyallup Valley is a great place to celebrate the advent of Spring as a magical world of color unveils over 150 varieties of daffodils, crocus, hyacinths and tulips. The Grand Floral Parade, each April, begins in Tacoma, and continues on to Puyallup, Sumner and Orting.

Fruit Salad & Lemon Dressing

Salad:
  3 ORANGES, peeled and sectioned
  2 BANANAS, sliced
  1 med. APPLE, chopped
  1 can (8 1/2 oz.) PINEAPPLE TIDBITS, drained

Dressing:
  1/2 cup SOUR CREAM   **1 tsp. LEMON EXTRACT**
  2 Tbsp. HONEY   **1/8 tsp. NUTMEG**
  1 tsp. VANILLA   **Dash of CINNAMON**

Garnish:
  TOASTED ALMONDS

In medium sized bowl, combine prepared fruit. Stir together sour cream, honey, extracts and spices. Combine dressing with fruits and toss lightly. Chill 30 minutes before serving. Garnish with almonds.

Apricot Nectar Gelatin Salad

Jimmie Holeman — Everett

4 1/2 cups APRICOT NECTAR
2 pkgs. (3 oz. ea.) LEMON GELATIN
8 oz. CREAM CHEESE

Dissolve gelatin in heated nectar. Place in dish and allow to set slightly. Meanwhile, make cream cheese into small balls. When the gelatin is slightly thickened, add the cream cheese balls. Refrigerate until firmly set.

Hot Seafood Salad

Arnie's Restaurants — Seattle, Edmonds and Mukilteo

Hot Sea Dressing:
3 EGG YOLKS
3/4 cup RED WINE VINEGAR
1/2 cup DIJON MUSTARD
2 Tbsp. HONEY
1 Tbsp. LEMON JUICE
3/4 tsp. KOSHER SALT
3/4 tsp. WHITE PEPPER
1/2 tsp. WORCESTERSHIRE
1/4 tsp. TABASCO®
3 cups SALAD OIL
1/3 cup WHITE ONION, minced

Seafood Salad (per serving):
8 oz. ROMAINE LETTUCE
1 oz. BACON, diced, raw
2 oz. SEA SCALLOPS
2 PRAWNS
2 oz. FRESH FISH (ling cod or rock fish, etc.)
1 oz. MUSHROOMS, sliced
1 oz. ZUCCHINI, diced
1 pinch THYME

6 oz. HOT SEA DRESSING
1 oz. TOMATO, diced
1/2 oz. PARMESAN CHEESE, grated
1/4 oz. GREEN ONIONS
1/2 oz. ALMONDS, toasted, sliced
1 LEMON WEDGE, garnish

Whip egg yolks in mixing bowl. Then, with mixer on low speed, add vinegar, mustard, honey, lemon juice, salt, pepper, Worcestershire and Tabasco. Slowly drizzle in salad oil until emulsified; add onion. Keep dressing refrigerated. Place romaine on salad plate. Sauté bacon on high until browned, then turn heat to medium and add seafood, mushrooms, zucchini and thyme. Sauté until seafood is thoroughly cooked, add hot sea dressing and tomatoes. Then remove from heat; pour over romaine and garnish with parmesan, green onions, almonds and lemon wedge in center.

Edmonds is the home of a historical museum, which includes a working shingle mill. Here, too, you will find the largest charter sport-fishing fleet on Puget Sound.

Main Dishes

Lemon Caper Chicken

Mt. Rainier Guest Services — Longmire

1 cup FLOUR
1/2 tsp. SALT
1 tsp. THYME
4 (3 oz. ea.) CHICKEN
    BREASTS, boneless,
    trimmed

1 1/2 oz. BUTTER
4 oz. WHITE WINE
1 LEMON, juiced
2 tsp. CAPERS
1 tsp. CHICKEN BASE

Mix flour, salt and thyme; then dredge chicken breast in flour mixture. Place butter in sauté pan and heat. Place breasts in pan and sauté until golden brown. Turn over and drain excess butter. Add white wine, lemon juice, capers and chicken base (make sure base dissolves to prevent from burning.) Reduce until sauce thickens. Place breast on plate and pour half of the sauce over each serving. Serves 2.

Longmire is located just inside the Nisqually entrance to Mount Rainier park, featuring a small museum, lodging and programs led by park rangers.

Sweet & Sour Chicken

Mae Holton, Jackson School — Everett

Coating the chicken:
- **1 cut-up FRYER**
- **1 or 2 EGGS, beaten**
- **1 cup CORNSTARCH**
- **1 tsp. GARLIC SALT**

Dip chicken in beaten eggs; combine cornstarch with garlic salt, coat the chicken pieces and fry in oil until golden brown.

Sauce:
- **1/4 cup CHICKEN BROTH**
- **1/4 cup CATSUP**
- **3/4 cup SUGAR**
- **1/2 cup VINEGAR**
- **1 Tbsp. SOY SAUCE**
- **1 tsp. SALT**

Combine ingredients and heat. Place chicken in baking dish. Pour hot sauce over all. Bake at 375 degrees for 1/2 hour or more, basting often.

Creole Chops

4 PORK RIB CHOPS
1 med. ONION, chopped
1 sm. GREEN PEPPER, sliced
2 tsp. PARSLEY FLAKES
1 tsp. SALT
1/2 tsp. PEPPER
1/8 tsp. GARLIC POWDER
1 can (16 oz.) STEWED TOMATOES
dash HOT PEPPER SAUCE
1 Tbsp. WORCESTERSHIRE SAUCE

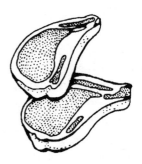

In a 10 inch skillet, brown chops on both sides over medium heat. Add remaining ingredients, and reduce heat. Cover tightly and simmer 30 minutes or until done.

Frank & Kraut Dinner

1 can CHEESE SOUP
1/4 cup MILK
1/2 tsp. CARAWAY SEED
1/2 tsp. PREPARED MUSTARD
1 can (27 oz.) SAUERKRAUT, drained and chopped
1 lb. WEINERS

   In small saucepan, combine soup with milk, stirring until well blended. Add caraway seeds and mustard. Fold in sauerkraut and heat through, stirring mixture often. Place in 10 x 6 x 1 1/2 inch baking dish. Cut each weiner on the diagonal at 1 inch intervals. Place on top of kraut and bake at 375 degrees, 15 to 20 minutes.

The Bavarian theme town of Leavenworth proudly displays alpine architecture, flower boxes and many restaurants of German and Austrian cuisine. Bands play "oom-pah-pah" music, and shops sell everything from cuckoo clocks to lederhosen. You may wonder if you have been transplanted to a mountain town in Europe!

Saucy Pork Chops

6 lg. PORK CHOPS, trimmed
GARLIC SALT, PEPPER to taste
1 lg. ONION, sliced
1 can CREAM OF CHICKEN SOUP
1 Tbsp. A-1® SAUCE
1/4 cup CATSUP
1 soup can MILK

   Brown pork chops in hot oil. Sprinkle with pepper and garlic salt to taste. Place pork chops in a 9 x 13, greased, baking dish. Cover with a layer of the sliced onion. Combine remaining ingredients and pour over the top. Bake at 350 degrees for one hour, adding water as needed.

Chili Meat Balls

Meat balls:
- **1 lb. GROUND BEEF**
- **2 EGGS**
- **18 SODA CRACKERS**
- **1/2 cup FRENCH DRESSING**
- **1/8 cup MILK**
- **1/2 cup WALNUTS, chopped**

Sauce:
- **1/2 sm. ONION, diced**
- **1 sm. GREEN PEPPER, diced**
- **1/2 cup CELERY, diced**
- **1 can TOMATOES**
- **1/2 tsp. CINNAMON**
- **1/2 tsp. CLOVES**
- **1/2 tsp. DRY MUSTARD**
- **1/4 cup VINEGAR**
- **1 cup BROWN SUGAR**

Combine ground beef, eggs, crushed crackers, dressing, milk and nuts. Mix well. Shape into meatballs; brown well in skillet. Place meatballs in casserole dish, cover with sauce, and bake 1 hour at 350 degrees. To make sauce, combine onions, green pepper and celery, add tomatoes and other ingredients and bring to a boil. Cook until tender.

Baked Drumsticks

2 cups CORN FLAKES
1/4 cup MARGARINE, melted
1/2 tsp. SALT
1/4 tsp. PEPPER
8 CHICKEN DRUMSTICKS

Place corn flakes into plastic bag and using a rolling pin, crush. Place crumbs into a pie plate. In a separate dish, melt margarine and stir in salt and pepper, mixing well. Rinse drumsticks and brush with melted margarine on all sides. Roll each piece into the crumbs until coated, and then place in a baking pan. If any margarine mixture remains, drizzle over chicken. Bake at 375 degrees for about 50 minutes, until done.

Old-Fashioned Meat Loaf

1 1/2 lbs. GROUND BEEF
3/4 cup QUICK OATS
1/4 cup ONION, chopped
1 1/2 tsp. SALT
1/4 tsp. PEPPER

1 EGG, beaten
3/4 cup MILK
1/3 cup CATSUP
1 Tbsp. MUSTARD
2 Tbsp. BROWN SUGAR

Combine first 7 ingredients in large bowl; mix well. Pat into loaf pan, bake at 350 degrees for 15 minutes. Remove from oven and drain. Combine remaining ingredients and place on top of meat loaf. Bake another 45 minutes.

Roslyn, Washington, where the television series "Northern Exposure" is filmed, has the greatest number of cemeteries of any city its size in the United States.

My Favorite Corned Beef Patties

Chris Fowler — Puyallup

2 cups FLOUR
1 tsp. BAKING POWDER
1/2 tsp. SALT
6 Tbsp. SHORTENING
1/3 to 1/2 cup MILK
1 EGG YOLK
Filling:
   2 Tbsp. MARGARINE, melted
   2 Tbsp. FLOUR
   1/2 cup ONION, diced
   1 1/2 to 2 cups CANNED TOMATOES
   1 can CORNED BEEF

Combine the dry ingredients and cut in shortening. With fork, gently stir in liquid and egg yolk. Roll on floured board, and cut into 12 squares. Combine filling ingredients and simmer 10 minutes. Line muffin tins with dough, spoon corned beef mixture in, and fold dough over top. Bake at 425 degrees for 20 minutes.

Four Bean Casserole

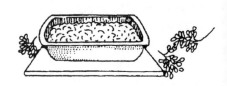

3/4 lb. BACON, diced, fried
4 lg. ONIONS, chopped, fried
1/3 cup VINEGAR
3/4 cup BROWN SUGAR
1 Tbsp. DRY MUSTARD
1 can LIMA BEANS
1 can KIDNEY BEANS
1 can PORK AND BEANS
1 can BUTTER BEANS

Cook together bacon, onions, vinegar, brown sugar and mustard. Simmer for 20 minutes, then add all beans. Bake in a large casserole dish for 2 hours at 325 degrees. Serves 10. (For a heartier dish, brown off 1 1/2 lb. of ground beef and add to above ingredients.

Chile Relleno Casserole

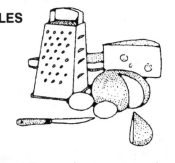

3 cans (7 oz. ea.) WHOLE GREEN CHILES
8 FLOUR TORTILLAS
1 lb. LOW-FAT CHEESE, grated
3/4 cup SKIM MILK
1/2 tsp. CUMIN
12 EGGS
1/2 tsp. PEPPER
1/2 tsp. GARLIC POWDER
1 tsp. PAPRIKA

Preheat oven to 300 degrees. Drain chiles and remove seeds. Spray 9 x 13 pan with non stick coating, and cut flour tortillas into 1 inch strips. Lay half the chiles in the pan, and top with half the tortilla strips and cheese. Repeat layers. Beat remaining ingredients, except paprika and pour over casserole. Sprinkle with paprika. Bake uncovered for 40 minutes, or until puffy, at 350 degrees. Let stand 10 minutes before serving.

Cajun Cornbread

Betty Fraine — Ellensburg

Cornbread:
  1 cup CORNMEAL
  1 scant cup FLOUR
  2 EGGS, well-beaten
  1/2 tsp. SODA
  3/4 tsp. SALT
  1 cup MILK
  1 can CREAMED CORN
  1/2 cup BACON DRIPPINGS

Combine all ingredients. Mix well and set aside.

Filling:
  1 1/2 lbs. GROUND BEEF
  1 large ONION, chopped
  1/2 lb. CHEDDAR CHEESE, grated
  JALAPEÑO PEPPERS, diced, to taste

Brown ground beef and onion together and drain; set aside. Grease a large cast-iron skillet. Pour half of the cornbread mixture into skillet and slowly brown on top of stove until it starts to set up. Spread layers of cheese, peppers and meat. Pour remainder of cornbread mixture on top. Bake at 350 degrees for 50 minutes. A complete meal with only a green salad needed. Serves 6-8.

Each September, Central Washington comes alive with the sights and sounds of one of the Northwest's great traditions, The Ellensburg Rodeo. Held at the same time as the annual fair, this city plays host to visitors from all over the state.

Super Simple Chuck Steak

Jennifer Knudson — Mukilteo

1 1/2 lbs. CHUCK STEAK
1 can CREAM OF MUSHROOM SOUP
1 env. DRY ONION SOUP MIX
3 med. CARROTS, quartered
2 stalks CELERY, cut in 2 inch pieces
3 med. POTATOES, pared, quartered
2 Tbsp. WATER

Heat oven to 450 degrees. Place 24 x 18 inch piece of heavy duty aluminum foil in a baking pan. Place meat on foil, then stir together mushroom soup and onion soup mix, spreading over meat. Top with vegetables, and sprinkle water over all. Fold foil over and seal securely. Bake 2 hours, or until tender.

Bellevue, Issaquah, Kirkland, Redmond and Woodinville are just a bridge away from Seattle, offering a city get-away including a salmon hatchery, tasty Swiss candies, festivals, wineries and lake cruises. About 30 miles to the east, Snoqualmie Falls is 100 feet taller than the more famous Niagara Falls.

Country Fried Pork Chops

4 PORK CHOPS
1 can (2 oz.) SLICED MUSHROOMS, drained
1 can CREAM OF CELERY SOUP
1/2 cup WATER
1/4 tsp. THYME, crushed
6 sm. WHOLE WHITE ONIONS
1 cup CARROTS, sliced

In skillet, brown chops and mushrooms in shortening. Pour off fat, then stir in soup, water and thyme. Add onions and carrots. Cover and cook over low heat for 45 minutes, or until tender.

Italian Shells Casserole

2 lbs. med. MACARONI SHELLS
2 lbs. LEAN GROUND BEEF
1 tsp. SALT
1/2 tsp. PEPPER
1 qt. MARINARA SAUCE
1 pt. SOUR CREAM
16 oz. PROVOLONE CHEESE, shredded
16 oz. MOZZARELLA CHEESE, shredded

Cook macaroni according to package until firm (al dente); rinse and drain. Brown ground beef in skillet, and add salt and pepper. Stir in marinara sauce and simmer 20 minutes. Using a deep lasagna pan or deep casserole dish, line the bottom with half the cooked shells. Cover the shells with half the meat sauce. Spread 1/2 pint of sour cream lightly over the sauce. Sprinkle with half of both cheeses. Repeat for second layer in same order. Cover and bake at 350 degrees for 40 minutes. Uncover and bake for 20 minutes more. The casserole is ready to serve when cheese is melted and lightly browned. Serves 8.

Ranging between Puget Sound and the Pacific, is Olympic National Park — 923,000 acres of natural scenic wilderness. Its highest point is Mount Olympus, at 7,965 feet. Rainfall averages 140 inches per year in the rain forests of the western valleys of the park. More than 6,500 elk inhabit the area.

Barbecued Chicken

1 CHICKEN, cut up
8 oz. FRENCH DRESSING
1 can CRANBERRY SAUCE
1 env. DRY ONION SOUP MIX

Heat together all ingredients, and pour over chicken. Bake at 375 degrees, 1 to 1 1/2 hours. Serves 6.

South of the Border Casserole

Gary James Knudson — Mukilteo

2 lbs. GROUND BEEF
1 ONION, chopped
1 clove GARLIC, minced
1 can (8 oz.) TOMATO SAUCE
dash PEPPER
3 Tbsp. CHILI POWDER
12 CORN TORTILLAS
1 can CREAM OF CHICKEN SOUP
3/4 cup MILK
2 cups CHEDDAR CHEESE, grated

Brown and drain beef. Add onion, garlic, tomato sauce, pepper and chili powder and simmer. Place six tortillas in bottom of 9 x 13 pan, and cover with meat mixture. Place remaining tortillas on top. Pour soup mixed with milk over them. Sprinkle with cheese. Bake at 350 degrees for 30 minutes. Serves 6.

Calico Ham Casserole

2 pkgs. FROZEN MIXED
    VEGETABLES
1/8 cup BUTTER
1 1/2 cups BREAD, cubed
3/8 cup BUTTER
1/2 cup FLOUR
1/8 tsp. PEPPER
1/2 tsp. SALT
1 tsp. DRY MUSTARD
1 tsp. WORCESTERSHIRE
    SAUCE
3 cups MILK
1 to 2 cups SHARP CHEDDAR
    CHEESE, grated
1/2 med. ONION, grated
1 lb. HAM, cooked, cubed

Prepare vegetables according to package, and drain. Set aside. Melt 1/8 cup butter and add to cubed bread. Toss with fork and set aside. Make a cream sauce with remaining butter, flour, seasonings, worcestershire sauce and milk. Add cheese to sauce and stir until cheese is melted over medium heat. When sauce is smooth, add onion, the set-aside vegetables and ham. Pour into a greased casserole and refrigerate overnight. Before baking, put the bread cubes that have been mixed with butter on top. Press down a little. Bake at 300 degrees for one hour. Serves 12.

Northwestern Ham Casserole

3 cups DICED HAM
1 pkg. (10 oz.) FROZEN LIMA BEANS, cooked
1 can (16 oz.) CREAM STYLE CORN
2 Tbsp. ONION, grated
1/2 tsp. MUSTARD
1 pkg. (8 1/2 oz.) CORN MUFFIN MIX

Combine the ham, beans, corn, onion and mustard, cooking slowly in saucepan until heated through. Pour into greased two quart baking dish. Prepare muffin mix as directed, and pour over top of ham mixture. Bake at 400 degrees until golden brown, about 20 to 25 minutes. Serves 6.

Campbell Country Chicken

The Campbell House — Chelan

2 oz. CLARIFIED BUTTER   **3 oz. SHERRY**
7 oz. CHICKEN BREAST, floured   **2 oz. CREAM**
pinch SHALLOTS   **pinch PARSLEY, chopped**
3 wedges GRANNY SMITH APPLE

Heat butter, add chicken (brown on both sides); season. Add shallots and apples, heat 30 seconds. Add sherry and reduce. Add cream and reduce to smooth consistency. Add parsley. Lay chicken on left side of plate, put apples on chicken and pour sauce on top. Serves 1.

The Campbell House was built in 1901, when the town of Chelan was nothing more than a village. Arriving from Iowa in 1889, C. C. Campbell purchased the site for $400. The seller later remarked at the local saloon that he had "just sold that sandpile to a sucker." The new hotel became a stopping place for teamsters and drivers. Cattle were driven across the Chelan River in those early days.

Crazy Crust Pizza

1 lb. GROUND BEEF, SAUSAGE
1/4 cup ONIONS, chopped
1 cup FLOUR
1 tsp. SALT
1/8 tsp. PEPPER
1 tsp. ITALIAN SEASONING
2 EGGS
2/3 cup MILK
1 cup PIZZA SAUCE
4 oz. can MUSHROOMS, drained
1 cup MOZZARELLA CHEESE, shredded

In a medium skillet, brown the ground meat and onions. Drain well and set aside. Lightly grease and dust a 12-14 inch pizza pan with flour. Prepare batter by mixing flour, salt, pepper, italian seasoning, eggs and milk in a small mixing bowl. Pour batter into pan, tilting pan until batter covers bottom. Arrange topping of meat and onions over batter. Bake on bottom oven rack at 425 degrees for 20-25 minutes, or until pizza is deep golden brown. Remove from oven, drizzle with pizza sauce, sprinkle with mushrooms, cheese and any other desired toppings. Return to oven for 10-15 minutes until cheese is melted and sauce is bubbly.

Flower lovers descend on Mount Vernon each spring, as hundreds of acres come alive with tulips, daffodils, and iris. Nearby Burlington has a new shopping mall and factory outlet stores to lure shoppers.

Hamburger Pizza

1 lb. GROUND BEEF
1 cup TOMATO SAUCE
1 cup CHEDDAR CHEESE or MOZZARELLA, grated

Flatten meat on cookie sheet. Broil 10 minutes. Season tomato sauce to your preference, and spread on top. Sprinkle with grated cheese and broil until cheese bubbles. Serves 4 to 6.

Zucchini Lasagna

Jennifer Knudson — Mukilteo

1 lb. ITALIAN SAUSAGE
1/2 cup ONION, chopped
1 can (15 oz.) TOMATO SAUCE
1/2 cup WATER
1/4 tsp. SALT
1/4 tsp. OREGANO
3/4 cup PARMESAN CHEESE, grated

2 Tbsp. FLOUR
6 LASAGNA NOODLES,
  cooked and drained
2 cups ZUCCHINI, sliced
12 oz. MOZZARELLA
  CHEESE, grated

Brown sausage and onion together and drain excess fat. Stir in tomato sauce, water, salt and oregano. Simmer 30 minutes, stirring occasionally. Meanwhile, in small bowl, combine parmesan cheese with flour. Grease 9 x 13 baking dish and lay 3 noodles on bottom. Top with zucchini, half of the parmesan mixture, half of the meat sauce and half of the grated mozzarella cheese. Repeat layers, except for mozzarella cheese. Bake at 375 degrees for 20-25 minutes until zucchini is tender. Then top with remaining mozzarella and return to oven until cheese begins to melt. Let stand 10 minutes, then serve.

Braised Short Ribs

1 med. ONION, chopped
1 1/2 Tbsp. BUTTER
1 1/2 Tbsp. VINEGAR
1 1/2 Tbsp. BROWN SUGAR
3/4 cup KETCHUP
3/4 cup WATER

1 1/2 tsp. SALT, divided
1 1/2 Tbsp. WORCESTERSHIRE
  SAUCE
1 1/2 tsp. DRY MUSTARD
3 1/2 to 4 lbs. SHORT RIBS

In medium saucepan, brown onion in butter. Add vinegar, brown sugar, ketchup, 1/2 tsp. water, salt, Worcestershire and mustard. Bring to a boil, reduce heat and simmer 10 minutes. Meanwhile, brown short ribs on all sides in large skillet or dutch oven, and drain off fat. Add sauce and remaining salt. Cover and bake at 300 degrees for 3 hours, or until tender, basting ribs with sauce 3 or 4 times during baking. Serves 4 to 6.

Sweet & Sour Meatballs

1 1/2 lbs. HAMBURGER

Form into small meatballs, brown in skillet and set aside.

Sauce:

1/2 cup **CELERY**, chopped	1/4 cup **VINEGAR**
1/3 cup **GREEN PEPPER**, chopped	1/3 cup **BROWN SUGAR**
1/4 cup **ONION**, chopped	1/2 tsp. **GINGER**
1 cup **CRUSHED PINEAPPLE**	2 Tbsp. **CORNSTARCH**
1 cup **CHICKEN BROTH**	1/3 cup **SOY SAUCE**

Combine all ingredients and heat to boiling. Place meatballs in casserole, pour sauce over all. Bake at 325 degrees about 30 minutes.

Red Beans Supreme & Rice

Norman B. Rice, Mayor, City of Seattle

1 sm. bag **RED BEANS**	**PEPPER**
6 **HAM HOCKS**	**BAY LEAVES**
1 med. **ONION**	**CELERY**
CHILI POWDER	**WORCESTERSHIRE**
SALT	

Wash and soak beans overnight, then rinse beans with boiling water before cooking. Place ham hocks in a pot of boiling water, cook until tender. Add red beans, sliced onion and other seasonings to taste, and mix well, simmering until done. The aroma will be over-powering and will cause mouth watering. Serve over a bed of rice. Cornbread muffins are excellent companion pieces for this hearty dish.

The Emerald City of Seattle was the sight of the 1962 World's Fair. Most of the original buildings are still standing, including the revolving restaurants atop the famous Space Needle. At your feet, you will have a 360 degree view of Mt. Rainier, the Olympics, Puget Sound, Pioneer Square, the Kingdome and all Seattle has to offer.

Sautéed Apples and Pork

Washington State Apple Commission — Wenatchee

1/2 cup plus 1 Tbsp. FLOUR, unsifted
1/2 tsp. SALT
1/2 tsp. GROUND BLACK PEPPER
4 (3 oz. ea.) PORK STEAKS, lean, boneless
3 Tbsp. BUTTER or MARGARINE
2 Tbsp. VEGETABLE OIL
2 GRANNY SMITH APPLES, peeled, cored, sliced
2 Tbsp. MINCED ONION
1 cup APPLE JUICE
1/2 cup DRY WHITE WINE
1/2 cup PLAIN YOGURT
2 Tbsp. DIJON MUSTARD
1/4 tsp. DRIED THYME LEAVES

In pie plate or shallow dish, combine 1/2 cup flour, 1/4 tsp. salt and 1/4 tsp. pepper; mix well. Dredge pork steaks in flour mixture to coat lightly. In large skillet, heat 2 Tbsp. butter and the oil over medium heat; add pork and cook until brown on both sides and juices run clear. Remove pork to heated platter and reserve. Add remaining butter to skillet, sauté apples and onions until both are tender. Remove to platter with pork. Add apple juice and wine to skillet, simmer 5 minutes. Combine yogurt, mustard, thyme, and remaining flour and salt; stir into juice mixture. Simmer 5 minutes, stirring until smooth. Spoon sauce over pork steaks and apples and serve. Serves 4.

Washington is the nation's top apple-producing state, accounting for more than half of all the apples eaten fresh in the United States. The apple was named the state's symbol in its Centennial year, 1989. Wenatchee and Yakima are the prime apple producing regions.

Rack of '37 House Lamb, Provençal

'37 House Bed and Breakfast — Yakima

4 to 5 lb. RACK OF LAMB (12 chops)	1 tsp. SALT
1 cup ITALIAN BREAD CRUMBS	1/4 tsp. PEPPER
1/4 cup chopped fresh PARSLEY	5 Tbsp. DIJON MUSTARD
3 cloves GARLIC, crushed	1/4 cup BUTTER, melted

Preheat oven to 375 degrees. Wipe lamb with damp paper towels. Trim off all fat. Place lamb, using ribs as rack, in shallow, open roasting pan. Roast, uncovered, 15 minutes for each pound. Remove roast from oven and let cool about 15 minutes. Combine bread crumbs, parsley, garlic, salt and pepper. Spread mustard over top of lamb. Pat crumb mixture into mustard, pressing firmly. Drizzle with butter. Roast 20 minutes. Garnish with parsley. Serves 6.

The Yakima Indian Reservation, just south of the city of Yakima is nearly twice the size of the state of Rhode Island.

Parmesan Chicken Fantastico

Nalley's Fine Foods — Tacoma

CHICKEN BREASTS, skinless, boneless
CHICKEN THIGHS, skinless
1/2 to 3/4 cup BERNSTEINS CHEESE FANTASTICO®
    SALAD DRESSING

Coating Mix:

1/4 cup PARMESAN CHEESE	1/2 tsp. PAPRIKA
3/4 cup TOASTED BREAD CRUMBS	SALT and PEPPER
2 Tbsp. PARSLEY, chopped, fresh	

Marinate chicken pieces in salad dressing for 1 hour or more, reserving marinade. In a heavy plastic bag, combine cheese, bread crumbs, parsley and paprika. Add salt and pepper to taste. Shake each chicken piece in bag of seasoned crumbs. Place in 9 x 13 pan, and spoon marinade over chicken pieces. Bake in 350 degree oven for 45-50 minutes.

Chicken Breast Dijon

Johnny's Dock Restaurant — Tacoma

2 (5 oz.) CHICKEN BREASTS, boneless, skinless
2 EGGS, well beaten
2 cups JAPANESE STYLE PANKO BREAD CRUMBS
1/2 tsp. SALT
2 pinches PEPPER
1 cup HEAVY CREAM
4 Tbsp. DIJON MUSTARD
1/2 tsp. CHICKEN BASE, granulated
1/4 tsp. CORNSTARCH
1 cup CANOLA OIL

Flatten and tenderize chicken breasts with a meat mallet. Dip prepared breasts into egg wash, coating lightly. Press breasts into panko crumbs. Season each breast with salt and pepper and refrigerate chicken until needed. In a bowl, mix cream, mustard, chicken base and cornstarch, being sure to dissolve the base and cornstarch completely. Cook the chicken in oil, on medium heat, until thoroughly cooked and golden brown. In a separate pan, on medium heat, reduce the dijon sauce until it thickens. Pour over chicken and serve with either fresh pasta or rice pilaf. Serves 2.

> *A great place to view sharks up close and watch playful whales jumping is the Point Defiance Park in Tacoma. In addition, the younger set enjoys elephant rides and it's also home to "Zoo Lights", a stunning light display, every Christmas.*

Elegant Meat Loaf

Jimmie Holeman — Everett

1 1/2 lbs. GROUND BEEF
1 EGG
1/2 cup ONION, chopped
1/2 cub BREAD CRUMBS
1/2 cup MILK
1 1/2 tsp. SALT
1/8 tsp. PEPPER
4 oz. CHEESE, sliced
2 TOMATOES, sliced

Combine first seven ingredients and place in 8 x 8 pan. Bake at 350 degrees for 25 minutes. Drain off fat, layer with cheese and tomato slices, then top with *Soufflé Topping* below.

Soufflé Topping

1 cup SOUR CREAM
3/4 cup FLOUR
3 EGGS, separated
1/2 tsp. SALT
1/8 tsp. PEPPER

Combine sour cream, flour, egg yolk, salt, and pepper in a small bowl. Beat until thick and creamy, then set aside. Beat egg whites until stiff. Fold egg whites into flour mixture and pour over cheese and tomato slices. Bake at 350 degrees, 30-40 minutes until golden brown. Cool 5 minutes before serving.

Swiss Steak

1 1/2 lb. ROUND STEAK
1/2 cup FLOUR
2 Tbsp. MELTED FAT
1 cup ONION, sliced
1 can (1 lb. 4 oz.) TOMATOES

1/2 cup CELERY, sliced
1 Tbsp. SUGAR
2 WHOLE CLOVES
1 1/2 tsp. SALT

Cover steak with flour, and pound into meat. Brown meat and onion slices in fat. Add tomatoes, celery, sugar, cloves and salt. Cover and cook over low heat or in 350 degree oven about 2 hours.

Northwestern Seafood

Seafood Newburg

Jimmie Holeman — Everett

1 pkg. (16 oz.) FROZEN COD, FLOUNDER or HADDOCK FILLETS
1 lb. med. SHRIMP or 12 oz. pkg. FROZEN SHRIMP,
    thawed, drained
1/4 cup MARGARINE
1/3 cup FLOUR
1 tsp. SALT
1/8 tsp. PEPPER
4 cups HALF & HALF
1 cup MILK
1 pkg. (10 oz.) FROZEN PEAS
1 pkg. (6 oz.) FROZEN CRAB MEAT, thawed
3/4 cup CHEESE, grated

Cut fish into bite size pieces and set aside. Melt margarine and stir in salt, flour and pepper. Cook 1 minute. Gradually stir in half & half and milk; then add peas, crab meat and its liquid, and prepared fish. Cook until fish is tender and it is slightly thickened. Add cheese, and sprinkle with a little paprika. Serve on biscuits, noodles or rice.

Baked Herb-Garden Salmon

Graham Kerr — Seattle

1 (4-6 pound) SALMON*, whole
1 tsp. LIGHT OLIVE OIL with a dash of toasted SESAME OIL
1 Tbsp. ALL-PURPOSE FLOUR, mixed with 1/8 tsp. SALT and
    1/8 tsp. freshly ground BLACK PEPPER
2 cloves GARLIC, crushed
1/8 tsp. SALT
1/8 tsp. freshly ground BLACK PEPPER
1 bunch fresh TARRAGON (or 1/2 tsp. dried)
1 bunch fresh ROSEMARY, intact if possible
1 bunch fresh THYME
1 bunch fresh DILL
1 whole LEMON, cut in 1/2 in. slices

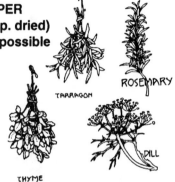

ROSEMARY
TARRAGON
DILL
THYME

Garnish:
    1 LEMON , cut into wedges
    ROSEMARY branches
    THYME sprigs
    DILL sprigs

Place salmon in cold water, remove scales and rinse. For a delicious, crispy skin, brush one side of the fish with the olive oil and work in well. Sprinkle with the flour and salt-and-pepper mixture, patting it firmly into the surface. Place fish on cutting board, prepared-side-up. Using the back of a knife, mark a lengthwise center guideline on the fish body, but do not cut the skin. Using a very sharp knife or razor blade, score diagonal incisions 1 inch apart from the top of the body down the center line almost to the belly. Make a final incision down the backbone so that the skin comes away easily when served.

Make a paste of the garlic, salt and pepper, and rub into incisions. Layer the herbs inside the fish. Lay the lemon slices down the center line.

Line a shallow baking pan with heavy-duty aluminum foil, shiny-side-up. Lift the prepared fish by the head and tail and place it so that the main body (at least) of the fish is in the pan. Wrap the head and tail in oiled aluminum foil. Be sure to fan the tail out so that it holds its shape.

Preheat the oven to 450°F. Bake the fish for 8 minutes per inch of thickness. Remove outer foil, switch oven to broil and pop the fish back in to crisp the skin for its table presentation, just until it blisters and browns (about 5 minutes).

To serve: Lift the fish out of the pan still on its aluminum-foil bed, place on a large oval serving plate and then slide the foil out from under the fish. Slice by following the skin lines, serving slices from the back and belly, garnished with pieces of the skin. Save pan drippings to drizzle over your side dishes for added taste.

When the top layer has been served (usually 6 portions), simply remove the head, the herbs and lemon wedges and pry up the backbone to reveal the remaining bone-free fillet.

Here is a Minimax method for cooking a whole fish. Using this technique you can cook any round-bodied whole fish: red snapper, large trout, striped bass, grouper, ocean perch, rockfish, pompano (bream), drum, mullet, or whitefish.

Baked Herb-Garden Salmon Plate

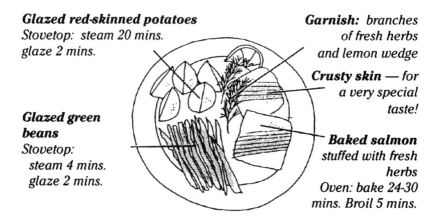

Glazed red-skinned potatoes
Stovetop: steam 20 mins.
glaze 2 mins.

Garnish: *branches of fresh herbs and lemon wedge*

Crusty skin — *for a very special taste!*

Glazed green beans
Stovetop:
steam 4 mins.
glaze 2 mins.

Baked salmon *stuffed with fresh herbs*
Oven: bake 24-30 mins. Broil 5 mins.

Copyright © 1993 by the Treena and Graham Kerr Corporation. Reproduced with permission from G. P. Putnam's Sons.

Shrimp Boil

Mike Lowry, Governor - State of Washington — Olympia

2 gal. WATER
12 BAY LEAVES
pinch of PEPPERCORN
1 tsp. MUSTARD SEED
1/2 tsp. BASIL
1/4 tsp. WHOLE CLOVES
pinch of CUMIN SEED
1 tsp. RED PEPPER
pinch of CELERY SALT
pinch of FENNEL SEED
pinch of CARAWAY SEED

1/8 tsp. GROUND MARJORAM
1/8 tsp. THYME LEAVES
1 sm. ONION
2 stalks CELERY
1/2 LEMON
2 Tbsp. SEA SALT
4 tsp. CAYENNE PEPPER
3 Tbsp. WORCESTERSHIRE SAUCE
1 cup WHITE WINE
60-70 THAWED SHRIMP
    (25-30 count per lb.)

Heat water to boiling. Add all seasonings, and coarsely chopped vegetables. Cook for 30 minutes. Add shrimp and cook for 5 minutes. Serve with *Cajun Sauce* below.

Cajun Sauce for Dipping

1/2 cup WINE VINEGAR
4 Tbsp. CREOLE MUSTARD
1 tsp. HORSERADISH
1 tsp. PAPRIKA
1 Tbsp. SALT

1 Tbsp. PEPPER
2 cups OLIVE OIL
1/4 cup chopped CELERY
3 chopped GREEN ONIONS
1/4 cup chopped PARSLEY

Combine vinegar with mustard, horseradish, paprika, salt and pepper. Gradually add olive oil while whipping vigorously. Add remaining finely minced ingredients.

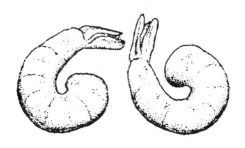

Lemon Mussels with Spinach Linguini

Captain Whidbey Inn — Coupeville

Mussel mixture:

5 lbs. MUSSELS, fresh, cleaned	1 BAY LEAF
1 cup ONION, chopped	dash of SALT
1 clove GARLIC, peeled, chopped	2 Tbsp. BUTTER
1/2 cup PARSLEY, chopped	1 cup DRY WHITE WINE

Sauce:

1/2 cup BUTTER, divided	2 cups MUSSEL BROTH
2 Tbsp. OLIVE OIL	12 oz. SPINACH LINGUINI
1 clove GARLIC, minced	2 Tbsp. PARMESAN
2 Tbsp. LEMON JUICE	LEMON WEDGES
2 tsp. LEMON PEEL, grated	1/4 tsp. PEPPER

Combine mussel mixture ingredients in a pot, cover, and place on high heat. Bring to a boil and cook 6 to 10 minutes. Remove mussels from pot and remove meat from shells. Pull off brown edge border around mussels and discard. Strain and reserve 2 cups broth. Heat 3 Tbsp. butter and olive oil in pan and sauté garlic. Add lemon juice, lemon peel, and broth, and simmer until liquid is reduced to about a cup. Add remaining butter; stir in mussels and heat. Cook spinach linguini and drain. Pour sauce over linguini and sprinkle with parmesan cheese. Serve with lemon wedges and crushed black pepper. *This recipe won the 1990 Penn Cove Mussel recipe contest.*

The Captain Whidbey Inn was built of madrona logs in 1907, on beautiful Whidbey Island. Joseph Whidbey was master of Captain Vancouver's flagship in 1792, when this island was discovered. Whidbey discovered a narrow passage at the north end of the island which he named Deception Pass. Today, visitors can cross Deception Pass Bridge as they travel to Whidbey Island, the 2nd largest island in the United States.

Oven Fried Snapper

2 lbs. SNAPPER FILLETS
1/2 cup OIL
1 tsp. SALT

2-3 cloves GARLIC, pressed
1 cup PARMESAN CHEESE
1 cup DRY BREAD CRUMBS

Rinse fish with cold water, pat dry with paper towels. Cut fish into six equal size serving portions. Combine the oil, salt and garlic in oblong glass baking dish. Place fish in mixture and let marinate ten minutes. Turn and marinate an additional ten minutes. Remove fish, roll in cheese, then in crumbs. Place on well greased cookie sheet. Bake at 500 degrees for 12-15 minutes, until fish flakes easily. Serves 6.

Smoked Salmon Tortellini

Johnny's Dock Restaurant — Tacoma

2 oz. MUSHROOMS, thinly sliced
1 oz. CANOLA or OLIVE OIL
1 oz. SALMON, kippered
1 oz. SALMON LOX
4 oz. TRI-COLOR TORTELLINI, cheese filled
1/2 oz. SCALLIONS, chopped
1 pinch SEAFOOD SEASONING
3 oz. FETTUCINI BASE
2 oz. PARMESAN CHEESE, freshly grated
1 bu. FRESH PARSLEY

Sauté the mushrooms in canola oil, add deboned kippered salmon and sliced salmon lox. Sauté together for about 30 seconds, add the pre-cooked tortellini, scallions, seafood seasoning and fettucini base. On medium heat, stir together and finish cooking until hot. Add half of the parmesan and melt together. After cooking, place in a proper sized dish and top with parmesan and chopped parsley. Serves 1.

Located near the newly remodeled Union Station, Johnny's Dock commands one of Tacoma's best views. It has been a landmark institution since 1947.

Coconut Prawns

Collectors Choice Restaurant — Snohomish

2 cups TEMPURA MIX
SEASONING MIX (recipe follows)
BEER
1/2 cup FLOUR
6 oz. COCONUT
20 PRAWNS
GREEN LEAF LETTUCE

Mix the tempura mix with 2 tsp. seasoning mix and enough beer to make tempura batter correct consistency. In small bowl, combine flour with seasoning mix (see below) and set aside. Place coconut in separate bowl. Sprinkle both sides of all prawns lightly with seasoning mix (4-5 tsp.). Hold prawns by tail to dip in flour mixture. Dip in tempura batter, allowing excess to drip off. Coat generously with coconut. Place on sheet pan and refrigerate until serving time. To serve: Deep fry at 350 degrees until golden brown. Place shrimp on green lettuce surrounding a bowl of *Sweet & Tangy Sauce.* Serves 4.

Seasoning Mix

1 tsp. CAYENNE
2 1/4 tsp. SALT
1 1/2 tsp. PAPRIKA
1 1/2 tsp. BLACK PEPPER

1 1/4 tsp. GARLIC POWDER
3/4 tsp. DRIED THYME
3/4 tsp. DRIED OREGANO

Combine well.

Sweet & Tangy Sauce

18 oz. ORANGE MARMALADE
5 Tbsp. BROWN MUSTARD
5 Tbsp. HORSERADISH

Combine, mix well, and ENJOY!

> Collectors Choice owners Donna and John Hager say, "Lots of prep time involved (1 hour). Time-consuming number of steps, but a delicious entree or appetizer. The spicy finished product is definitely worth the effort."

Deep Dish
Salmon-Potato Pie

Collectors Choice Restaurant — Snohomish

2 lbs. POTATOES, thinly sliced
4 CARROTS, peeled and thinly sliced
3 med. ONIONS, thinly sliced
4 Tbsp. BUTTER
1 can (15 oz.) SALMON, drained, boned
1 EGG YOLK
SINGLE PIE CRUST

Preheat oven to 300 degrees. Grease well a 2 qt. oval casserole or baking dish. In small amount of boiling water, cook potatoes and carrots 10 minutes and then drain. Sauté onion in 2 Tbsp. butter for 5 minutes. In prepared casserole, layer half of potatoes, carrots, onions, and salmon. Top with half of *Salmon Pie Sauce.* Repeat layering with remaining potatoes, carrots, onions, sauce and salmon. Dot with remaining 2 Tbsp. butter. Roll dough to 14 x 10 oval. Cut three 2-1/2 inch rounds with cookie or biscuit cutter and reserve. Fit pastry over pie, and brush top with some of yolk mixture. Cut rounds in half. Arrange on top of pastry, brush and flute edges. Bake 30 minutes. This is a hearty lunch, or a light dinner. Serves 8.

Salmon Pie Sauce

1/4 cup BUTTER
1/3 cup FLOUR
2 1/2 tsp. SALT

2 cups MILK
1/4 tsp. PEPPER
1/8 tsp. PAPRIKA

Melt butter. Stir in flour, salt, pepper and paprika. Blend in milk and heat until thickened.

Grilled King Salmon

Edgewater Inn — Seattle

1 (6 oz.) SALMON FILLET, for each serving
PICKLED ASPARAGUS
STRAWBERRIES

Grill salmon to your liking, set on top of a bed of wild greens, garnish with pickled asparagus and strawberries. The final touch is the drizzle of the *Marionberry Vinaigrette* on top.

Marionberry Vinaigrette

2/3 cup SUGAR
1 cup BALSAMIC VINEGAR
1/4 cup SHALLOTS, minced
2 Tbsp. ROSEMARY, chopped
1/4 cup WALNUT OIL
1/2 cup VEGETABLE OIL
3 cups MARIONBERRIES (or raspberries)
SALT to taste
BLACK PEPPER to taste

Dissolve sugar into vinegar, using a whisk. Add shallots and rosemary. Slowly add oils by drizzling them very slowly into the vinegar while using a whisk to emulsify the dressing. Add berries after the oil is emulsified, and using your whisk, crush some of the berries into the dressing to give texture and flavor. Season.

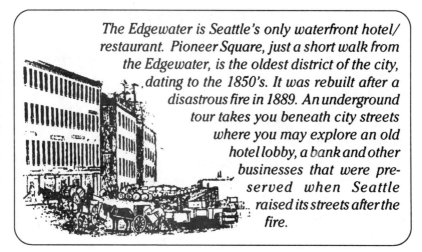

The Edgewater is Seattle's only waterfront hotel/restaurant. Pioneer Square, just a short walk from the Edgewater, is the oldest district of the city, dating to the 1850's. It was rebuilt after a disastrous fire in 1889. An underground tour takes you beneath city streets where you may explore an old hotel lobby, a bank and other businesses that were preserved when Seattle raised its streets after the fire.

Hot Crab Soufflé

Debbie Nielsen — Marysville

**10 slices WHITE BREAD (crusts removed and cut into
    small squares)**
2 cups CRAB or 2-1/2 cups CHICKEN or TURKEY, cooked, diced
1 cup CELERY, finely chopped
1 sm. ONION, finely chopped
1/2 cup MAYONNAISE
1/2 GREEN PEPPER, optional
4 EGGS
3 cups MILK
1 can MUSHROOM SOUP (if making seafood soufflé), - OR -
**   1 can CREAM OF CHICKEN SOUP (if making chicken soufflé)**
2 cups CHEDDAR CHEESE, grated
1 cup POTATO CHIPS, finely crushed, (optional)
PAPRIKA

Place half of bread squares in buttered 9 x 13 baking dish. Mix seafood (or chicken/turkey) with celery, onion and mayonnaise; spread over bread. Cover with remaining bread. Beat eggs and milk and pour over mixture. Refrigerate overnight. Bake at 350 degreees for 15 minutes. Remove from oven, spoon soup over top. Top with cheese and potato chips; garnish with paprika. Bake one hour longer at 325 degrees. Serves 8 to 10.

Clam Soufflé

10 to 12 SODA CRACKERS
1 cup COLD MILK
2 EGGS, beaten
SALT and PEPPER
1/4 cup BUTTER or MARGARINE, melted
1 can MINCED CLAM

Break crackers into small pieces and cover with milk. Let stand about 30 minutes. Stir eggs, salt and pepper (to taste) into cracker mixture; add butter and clams. Blend and pour into buttered casserole. Bake at 350 degrees about 45 minutes, until casserole is nicely browned on top.

Ocean Crest Seafood Soufflé

Ocean Crest Dinner House — Moclips

12 slices BREAD
4 cups BAY SHRIMP
2 cups CRAB MEAT
1 GREEN PEPPER, chopped fine
1 1/2 cup CELERY, chopped fine
1 lg. ONION, chopped fine
1/4 cup MAYONNAISE

7 EGGS
5 cups MILK or HALF & HALF
1 can CREAM OF MUSHROOM
   SOUP
2 cups CHEDDAR CHEESE,
   grated

Trim the crusts off the bread, set aside 8 slices. Cut the remaining 4 slices into small cubes, and place in a greased oblong cake pan. Combine the shrimp, crab meat, green peppers, celery and onion with the mayonnaise. Spread evenly over cubed bread. Top with the 8 slices of bread. Now, beat eggs and milk; pour slowly over soufflé. Refrigerate overnight. Cover the top with the soup, then sprinkle cheese on top. Bake at 325 degrees, 40-50 minutes. Serves 16.

Seafood Fettucini

Collectors Choice Restaurant — Snohomish

1 to 2 Tbsp. CLARIFIED
   BUTTER
FLOUR
3 oz. COD PIECES
21 to 25 PRAWNS
1 tsp. MINCED GARLIC
1/2 tsp. SALT
1/4 tsp. WHITE PEPPER
1 to 2 oz. WHITE WINE

4 oz. BAY SHRIMP, cooked
2 to 3 oz. DUNGENESS CRAB
   LEGS, cooked, shelled
4 oz. HEAVY CREAM
12 oz. FETTUCINI NOODLES,
   cooked (or other pasta)
PARMESAN CHEESE
MINCED FRESH DILL or
   DRIED DILL

Heat sauté pan and add clarified butter. Flour cod and prawns and add to sauté pan, sauté and turn. Add minced garlic, salt and white pepper, and sauté until garlic turns white. Deglaze with white wine and sauté 1 minute longer. Add bay shrimp, crab legs, heavy cream, and cooked pasta. Sauté until heated through and season to taste. Place on plates and garnish with parmesan cheese and dill. Great with fresh greens and garlic bread. Serves 2.

Westport Seafood Fettucini

Ocean Crest Dinner House — Moclips

1/2 oz. COOKING OIL
1 lg. pinch of GARLIC
1 1/2 oz. MUSHROOMS, sliced
3 oz. WHITE FISH, cubed
1 oz. BABY PRAWNS
2 oz. SCALLOPS
1 oz. SHRIMP
1 oz. CRAB MEAT

2 oz. FETTUCINI
3/4 oz. GREEN ONIONS
1/3 cup SOUR CREAM
1/4 cup HALF & HALF
1 1/2 oz. PARMESAN, grated
SEASONING SALT
SWEET BASIL, large pinch

Heat oil in sauté pan and add garlic, mushrooms, and fish; sauté 1 minute. Add baby prawns and scallops; sauté 1-2 minutes more. Add shrimp, crab meat, fettucini, green onions, sour cream and half & half, sauté until heated through. Finish off with the parmesan cheese, and add seasonings. Serve in a large heated boat, sprinkling top with fresh, chopped parsley, if desired.

Salmon Croquettes

1 can (16 oz.) SALMON, drained
1 EGG
1/4 cup BREAD CRUMBS

White Sauce:

1 Tbsp. FLOUR
1 Tbsp. MARGARINE
1 1/2 cups MILK
pinch PARSLEY FLAKES
pinch OREGANO

1/2 tsp. SALT
1/4 tsp. PEPPER
1/4 cup MUSHROOMS, sliced
1/4 cup ONIONS, chopped

Flake the salmon and add egg and bread crumbs, mixing lightly. Shape into croquettes. Roll croquettes into additional bread crumbs and deep fry. Accompany with white sauce. To make white sauce, combine flour and margarine over low heat. Add milk, and cook quickly stirring constantly. Add parsley, oregano, salt and pepper. Sauté mushrooms and onions in additional margarine. Add this mixture to the white sauce. Place croquettes in serving dish, pouring white sauce over them. Sprinkle with additional parsley flakes for color, if desired.

Baked Scallops with Sautéed Apples

Washington Apple Commission

6 slices BACON, halved crosswise
12 lg. SEA SCALLOPS (about 1 lb.)
2 Tbsp. BUTTER
2 GOLDEN DELICIOUS APPLES, cored, cut into 8 wedges each
1/8 tsp. SUGAR
1/2 cup APPLE CIDER
1 Tbsp. LEMON JUICE
SALT and PEPPER

Preheat oven to 425 degrees. In large skillet, sauté bacon over medium-low heat just until it renders fat, but does not brown (about 4 minutes). Transfer bacon to a piece of paper towel to drain. Wipe out skillet to remove drippings. Lightly butter a shallow baking dish. Arrange scallops in a single layer. Arrange the bacon on top of scallops and bake just until the bacon browns, and the scallops are cooked (about 10 minutes). Meanwhile, in the skillet, melt butter over medium heat; add apple slices and sugar. Sauté, stirring and turning, until apples are golden (5-6 minutes). Spoon off 2 tablespoons of juice from baked scallops and add to apples along with apple cider and lemon juice. Heat, stirring gently, over high heat until the juices boil, thicken slightly and coat the apple slices. Season with salt and pepper as desired. To serve, arrange bacon-topped scallops on 4 dinner plates. Arrange four apple slices, fanned, on each plate. Spoon skillet juices over scallops and apples; serve immediately. Serves 4.

"A quick, easy and elegant creation that won't cause any stress in the kitchen."

"Bug" was suggested as the name for one Washington town, but when local women objected, it was named "Sedro" (Spanish for cedar). In 1889, P. A. Woolley platted a town nearby, and the two towns combined to become Sedro Woolley. It is the western gateway to Cascade National Park and the town of Winthrop, now renovated into an "Old West" town.

Onion-Crusted Fillet of Salmon

The Apple Growers of Washington State

Red Onion Vinaigrette:

16 oz. PICKLED BEETS
1 cup RED WINE
1/2 cup RICE WINE VINEGAR
4 RED ONIONS (2 lbs.), sliced
2 cloves GARLIC, chopped
2 Tbsp. OLIVE OIL
2 Tbsp. PICKLING SPICE
(tied in cheesecloth)

2 Tbsp. SUGAR
1 tsp. BLACK PEPPER
2 sprigs fresh ROSEMARY
2 CINNAMON STICKS
2 Tbsp. CORNSTARCH,

Onion-crusted Fillet of Salmon:

4 lg. YELLOW ONIONS, finely minced
4 (6 oz.) SALMON FILLETS
2 Tbsp. OLIVE OIL
SALT and PEPPER

Salad of Apples and Beets:

2 GOLDEN DELICIOUS APPLES,
cut in 1/2 inch chunks
1 CUCUMBER, peeled,
seeded, diced
2 Tbsp. chopped CORIANDER

1 cup RICE WINE VINEGAR
2 Tbsp. LEMON JUICE
1/2 cup PICKLED BEETS,
cut in julienne

Drain and measure 1 cup liquid from pickled beets and pour into large saucepan. Add wine, vinegar, red onions, garlic, oil, pickling spice, sugar (dissolved in 2 Tbsp. water), pepper, rosemary and cinnamon sticks. Bring to simmer, cook about 15 minutes, or until reduced by one third. Remove and discard cinnamon and pickling spice, and purée remaining mixture in blender. Return to saucepan and stir in cornstarch mixture. Bring to boil, stirring, and cook until slightly thickened. Heat oven to 350 degrees. Lightly grease two baking sheets. Spread minced onion in thin layer on one baking sheet and bake until slightly brown. Cool on sheet. Season salmon to taste; brush fillets lightly with olive oil. Top each with a 'crust' of browned onion and place on greased sheet. Bake 10-12 minutes or until fish flakes slightly, and appears cooked through. In medium-sized bowl, combine apples, cucumber and chopped coriander. Drizzle with vinegar and lemon juice and toss to blend. Just before serving, sprinkle pickled beets on top. To serve, cover bottom of plate with vinaigrette, top with fillet and add salad. Serves 4.

Halibut Provençal

Canlis Restaurant — Seattle

4 (6 oz.) HALIBUT (or SOLE or COD) fillets
4 pieces PARCHMENT PAPER (or foil), approximately 12" round
1 AVOCADO, diced
8 oz. SHRIMP MEAT
12 BAY SCALLOPS
4 Tbsp. CRAB MEAT

For each portion, lay a piece of halibut onto paper, folded in half. Top with mixed seafood and avocado, spoon 3 Tbsp. of the prepared *Tomato Sauce* mix (below) over top. Wrap in parchment paper by folding edges, sealed like pie dough. Parchment paper is available at all cooking stores, and makes the best presentation. Preheat oven to 450 degrees, then reduce heat to 400, and bake for 20 minutes. To serve at the table, simply cut the paper around the edge, fold back and serve in the paper. You may use foil, making sure to wrap loosely with plenty of room to steam. Remove fish from foil before serving. Serve with rice pilaf.

Tomato Sauce

2 TOMATOES, chopped fine
1/4 cup BASIL, sliced very thin
1/4 cup ZUCCHINI, sliced thin
1/2 ONION, chopped fine
1/4 cup MUSHROOMS, sliced thin
1/4 cup RED PEPPER, sliced thin
1/4 cup GREEN PEPPER, sliced thin

Season with garlic (use plenty because a nice garlic flavor enhances this dish), spices of Provence (thyme, oregano, basil, bay and lavender), salt and pepper to taste. Sauté ingredients in 4 oz. of butter for 4 to 5 minutes. Strain and cool. (Enough sauce for 4 servings.)

Grilled Salmon in Sorrel Sauce

Janot's Bistro — Anacortes

1 bunch SORREL, cleaned,
   stemmed, chopped
1/2 tsp. SHALLOTS, minced
1 oz. BUTTER
2 oz. WHITE WINE

1 cup WHIPPING CREAM
pinch SALT
pinch WHITE PEPPER
2 SALMON STEAKS
   or FILLETS

Cook sorrel and shallots in a sauce pan with butter, mashing the sorrel with a whip or spoon. Add white wine and reduce by half. Add the cream and reduce by half again, or until sauce consistency. Strain sauce through a fine sieve, pressing as much of the pulp through as possible. Season with salt and pepper. Grill salmon. Place sauce on plate and salmon on top. Serves 2.

Steamer Clams with Curry & Basil

Janot's Bistro — Anacortes

1 lb. MANILA CLAMS, small, washed well
1 tsp. SHALLOTS, chopped
1 tsp. GARLIC, chopped
1 tsp. CURRY POWDER
1 tsp. FRESH BASIL, fine julienne cut
1/4 oz. LEEK, fine julienne cut
1/4 oz. CARROT, fine julienne cut
1/4 oz. CELERY, fine julienne cut
1 cup WHITE WINE
SALT and PEPPER to taste

Place all ingredients in a sauce pot with a lid. Bring to a boil and simmer until clams open. Place in bowl and serve immediately. Serves 2.

Side Dishes

Half Stuffed Baked Potato

Canlis Restaurant — Seattle

3 lg. BAKED POTATOES
SALT, PEPPER to taste
3 Tbsp. ROMANO CHEESE, ground
2 Tbsp. (heaping) GREEN ONION, chopped
4 oz. BUTTER
WHITE PEPPER to taste
3 Tbsp. BACON, chopped, fried
3 Tbsp. (heaping) SOUR CREAM

Spoon out the meat of the potatoes and mix well with the above ingredients, saving some Romano for topping. Put mixture back into potato shells. Stick one pat of butter in either end of the potato. Sprinkle with Romano and paprika. Heat through in 400 degree oven for one hour. May be prepared the day before needed, covered with plastic wrap, and refrigerated. Pop in oven when ready to use.

The Canlis is one of Seattle's finest restaurants featuring kimono-clad waitresses and an outstanding view of Lake Union and the Cascade Mountains.

Mexican Corn

American Fine Foods, canners of Walla Walla® vegetables

2 EGGS, beaten
1 cup CORNMEAL
1 can (17 oz.) CREAM CORN
1/4 cup mild SALSA
1/3 cup MARGARINE, melted
1/2 tsp. BAKING SODA
1/2 tsp. SALT
1/3 lb. CHEDDAR CHEESE, grated
1 can (4 oz.) DICED GREEN CHILES

In a bowl, combine eggs, corn meal, corn, salsa, margarine, baking soda and salt. Place half the mixture in the bottom of a greased casserole dish and top with half the cheese. Then add the chiles. Repeat with remaining corn mixture and remaining cheese. Bake, uncovered, at 350 degrees for 45 minutes.

Green Bean Casserole Parmesan

American Fine Foods, canners of Walla Walla® vegetables

1 can (16 oz.) SLICED GREEN BEANS, well-drained
1 can (16 oz.) BEAN SPROUTS, well-drained
1 can (5 oz.) WATER CHESTNUTS, drained and sliced
1 can (4 oz.) SLICED MUSHROOMS, drained
1/4 cup GRATED PARMESAN CHEESE
3 Tbsp. BUTTER, melted
1 can (8 oz.) TOMATO SAUCE
1/2 tsp. SALT
1 can (3 1/2 oz.) FRENCH FRIED ONION RINGS

Toss vegetables with parmesan cheese in an 8 x 12 inch shallow baking dish. Drizzle with melted butter. Combine tomato sauce and salt; pour over vegetables. Sprinkle onion rings on top. Bake in preheated oven at 325 degrees for 20 minutes. Serves 6.

Roasting Walla Walla Sweets & Potatoes

3 lg. WALLA WALLA SWEET ONIONS
3-4 med. RUSSET POTATOES
2 Tbsp. VEGETABLE OIL
1/4 tsp. SALT
1/8 tsp. BLACK PEPPER

Halve each onion lenthwise through the top and root, then skin, peeling away any slippery membrane. Dig into center of each half with a metal spoon, and scoop out flesh, leaving a 1/2 inch thick shell. Chop enough of the inner flesh to measure 2 cups and set aside. Scrub potatoes and cut enough of the potatoes into 1/4 to 1/2 inch dices to make 4 cups. Heat oil in large skillet, adding chopped onion and potatoes, salt and pepper. Sauté over medium high heat, stirring occasionally, about 5 minutes until onion begins to soften. Arrange 6 scooped-out halves in large greased baking dish. Spoon about 1/2 cup of potato mixture into each onion shell, then arrange remaining potato mixture all around them in a layer no deeper than 1 inch. Bake in 375 degree oven for 1 hour, until potatoes are thoroughly cooked and deeply browned. Serves 6.

Walla Walla Sweets were introduced here in the late 1800's by Peter Pieri, who brought the original seed stock from the Isle of Corsica. Make the most of them during their season (June-August), because their high moisture and sugar content make them very fragile. They have a shelf life of only 2 to 3 weeks after harvest.

Stuffed Walla Walla Sweets

4 WALLA WALLA SWEET ONIONS
3 Tbsp. BUTTER
1/4 lb. MUSHROOMS, finely chopped
1 cup CELERY, finely chopped
12 oz. PORK SAUSAGE
1 cup SOFT BREAD CRUMBS
1/4 tsp. SALT
1/4 tsp. PEPPER
3/4 cup CHICKEN BROTH
3/4 cup DRY WHITE WINE or DRY SHERRY

Trim roots of onions, then skin and peel off any slippery membrane. Cut off tops and dig into center with a metal spoon. Scoop out flesh, leaving 1/4 inch shell. Chop enough flesh to measure 2 cups. Melt butter in large pot, adding chopped onions, mushrooms and celery; sauté until softened. Meanwhile, sauté sausage until barely brown. With slotted spoon, add sausage to vegetable mixture, along with bread crumbs, salt and pepper. Spoon stuffing into onion shells. Place in shallow dish and pour on broth and wine. Cover loosely with foil and bake in 400 degree oven for 20 minutes, reduce temperature to 350 degrees and cook 25 minutes more. Remove foil and bake uncovered for up to 30 minutes until they are brown. Baste frequently during final stages to keep moist. Pour remaining liquid over them to serve.

Walla Walla, the town accused of having been named twice so as not to forget its name, is home to the Walla Walla Onion Festival in July. Nearby Dayton is home to Washington's oldest (built in 1881) remaining railroad station. To the north, climbing 2,000 feet out of the Snake River Country from Clarkston, you arrive at the world's richest dryland wheat country, known as the "Palouse". Pullman is the largest community there, home to Washington State University.

Creamed Onions

3 lbs. sm. WHITE ONIONS
2 qts. BOILING WATER
1/4 cup MARGARINE
3 Tbsp. FLOUR

1/4 tsp. NUTMEG
1/8 tsp. PEPPER
1 cup HEAVY CREAM
1/2 tsp. SALT

In boiling water, blanch unpeeled onions until outer skins wrinkle. Drain, and when cool, clip off skins and trim root ends. Cook onions in the water, covered, for 10 minutes or until fork tender. Drain, reserving water. Melt margarine in sauce pan, stirring in flour, nutmeg and pepper. Add cream, and 1 cup of the onion water. Cook, stirring constantly, 3 minutes or until thickened and smooth, with no raw flour taste. Stir in salt, and return onions to pan. Heat 2 to 3 minutes in sauce. Pour into serving dish, sprinkle with nutmeg.

Swiss Vegetable Medley

1 bag FROZEN BROCCOLI, CARROTS, and CAULIFLOWER
   combination, thawed and drained
1 can CREAM OF MUSHROOM SOUP
1 cup SWISS CHEESE, shredded
1/3 cup SOUR CREAM
1/4 tsp. PEPPER
4 oz. PIMIENTO, chopped, drained
1 can (2.8 oz.) FRENCH FRIED ONION RINGS

Combine vegetables, soup, 1/2 cup cheese, sour cream, pepper, pimiento and 1/2 can onion rings. Pour into a 1 quart casserole. Bake covered 30 minutes at 350 degrees. Top with remaining cheese and onion rings. Bake uncovered 5 minutes longer.

Squash Supreme

2 cups YELLOW SQUASH,
   cooked, drained
1 cup SOUR CREAM
1 can CREAM OF CHICKEN SOUP

1 CARROT, grated
1 ONION, chopped
1 pkg. HERB STUFFING
SALT, PEPPER to taste

Cook and drain squash, and add next 5 ingredients. Butter a casserole dish, and place a layer of stuffing on the bottom. Top with squash mixture. Repeat, ending with stuffing on top. Dot with butter, and bake at 350 degrees for 30 to 35 minutes. Serves 8.

Zucchini Cheddar Bake

Mae Holton — Everett

6 cups ZUCCHINI
SALT to taste
1 1/2 cups SHREDDED CHEESE
6 slices BACON, cooked, drained
2 EGG YOLKS, beaten

1 cup SOUR CREAM
2 Tbsp. FLOUR
2 EGG WHITES,
   stiffly beaten
1/4 cup BREAD CRUMBS

Simmer squash until tender, drain and sprinkle with salt. Place half the squash in a 7 x 12 pan, top with half the cheese and all the crumbled bacon. Combine egg yolks, sour cream and flour. Fold egg whites in yolk mixture. Repeat layers. Melt small amount of butter, mix with bread crumbs; sprinkle on top. Bake at 350 degrees until set.

Broccoli Casserole

2 pkgs. FROZEN BROCCOLI, chopped
1 EGG, slightly beaten
1/2 cup MAYONNAISE
1 sm. ONION, chopped
1 can CREAM OF MUSHROOM SOUP
1 cup CHEDDAR CHEESE, grated
1/2 pkg. HERB STUFFING MIX
1/4 cup BUTTER, melted

Cook broccoli slightly less than package directs. Mix broccoli, egg, mayonnaise, onion, soup and cheese in a greased 2-quart casserole. Mix stuffing with butter and sprinkle over broccoli. Bake at 350 degrees for 30 minutes.

Creamy Spinach

1 pkg. (10 oz.) FROZEN
   CHOPPED SPINACH
1 1/2 cups SOUR CREAM

1 envelope ONION SOUP MIX
1/3 cup PARMESAN CHEESE
4 slices BACON

Thaw and drain spinach and place in greased casserole. Combine sour cream, onion soup mix and parmesan cheese. Place on top of spinach. Lay slices of bacon over top, and bake at 375 degrees about 30 minutes.

Buffet Potatoes

1 ONION, chopped
1/2 cup FLOUR
4 cups LIGHT CREAM
1 tsp. SALT
1/4 tsp. TABASCO®
1/2 tsp. MARJORAM
1/2 lb. CRISP BACON, crumbled
1/2 lb. SWISS CHEESE, grated
8 large POTATOES, boiled and cubed

Sauté onion in small amount of fat; then add flour, cream, salt, Tabasco and marjoram stirring until thickened. When sauce has come to a boil, add bacon and swiss cheese. Place potatoes in buttered casserole dish, pouring sauce over, and baking at 350 degrees until heated through. Serves 8.

Potatoes are one of the main farm crops grown in the beautiful Skagit Valley, near Mount Vernon. It is also one of the largest daffodil and tulip bulb-growing areas in the world. The stunning flowers may be celebrated during the Skagit Tulip Festival each April.

Hash Brown Casserole

1 pint SOUR CREAM
1 can CREAM OF CHICKEN SOUP
2 Tbsp. DRIED ONION FLAKES
1/2 cup MARGARINE, melted
2 lb. FROZEN HASH BROWNS, thawed, cubed
2 cups CHEDDAR CHEESE, grated
2 cups CORN FLAKES, crushed
1/4 cup MARGARINE, melted and cooled

Combine sour cream, soup, onion flakes and the 1/2 cup of melted margarine and set aside. Lightly stir together the potatoes and grated cheese, adding to the sour cream mixture. Then, place in a buttered 9 x 13 casserole dish. Combine the corn flakes and the cooled margarine, mixing with a fork. Sprinkle over top, and bake at 350 degrees for 45-60 minutes.

Breads

Oatmeal Raisin Bread

Rev. Willis Walker — Yakima

1 1/2 cups WATER, boiling
1 cup OATS
1/2 cup MOLASSES
1/3 cup MARGARINE or
    SHORTENING
1 Tbsp. SALT

2 pkgs. DRY YEAST
1/2 cup WATER, warm
2 EGGS
5 1/2 cups FLOUR, sifted
1 cup RAISINS

Combine water, oats, molasses, margarine and salt. Stir well and cool until lukewarm. Meanwhile, soften the yeast in 1/2 cup warm water. Beat eggs and combine with softened yeast. Stir into cooled oat mixture, adding raisins last. Gradually add flour, and mix until well blended. Place dough in greased bowl, cover and refrigerate for at least 2 1/2 hours. When chilled, shape into two loaves and place in greased bread pans. Cover and let rise in a warm place until double in size, about 2 hours. Bake at 350 degrees for one hour.

Pineapple-Nut Upside Down Muffins

1/4 cup BROWN SUGAR, firmly packed
2 Tbsp. MARGARINE, melted
12 PECAN or WALNUT HALVES
1 1/4 cups FLOUR
3 1/2 tsp. BAKING POWDER
1 tsp. SALT
1/3 cup SUGAR
1 1/2 cups 40% BRAN FLAKES® CEREAL
1 can (8 oz.) CRUSHED PINEAPPLE, undrained
1/4 cup MILK
1 EGG
1/4 cup OIL
1/2 cup NUTS, coarsely chopped

Combine brown sugar and margarine. Portion scant teaspoon into each of twelve greased muffin pan cups. Place nut half in each. Stir together flour, baking powder, salt and sugar and set aside. In large mixing bowl, measure bran flakes, pineapple and milk, mixing well. Let stand about two minutes, then add egg and oil and beat well. Stir in chopped nuts, and add flour mixture, stirring only until combined. Batter will be thick. Portion evenly into muffin pan cups, and bake at 400 degrees for about 25 minutes, until browned. Serve warm.

Overnight Yeast Rolls

Evelyn Hayes — Everett

4 cups WATER
1 1/2 cups SUGAR
1 cup LARD or OIL
4 EGGS, beaten

1 Tbsp. SALT
1 pkg. DRY YEAST
13 cups FLOUR

At noon, boil water and sugar for 5 minutes, then add lard. At 3:30 p.m., add eggs, salt, yeast, water and flour. Raise till 6 p.m. and punch down. About 10 p.m., shape into rolls and put into greased pans, letting set overnight. Bake at 350 degrees until done (about 15 minutes).

Groveland's Dried Fruit Scones

Simone's Groveland Cottage Bed & Breakfast — Sequim

10 dried APRICOTS	**2 cups FLOUR**
6 DRIED PITTED PRUNES	**1 tsp. SUGAR (optional)**
2 Tbsp. BAKING POWDER	**1 1/4 cup HEAVY CREAM**

In a food processor, chop the apricots, adding the prunes and chop just briefly. Add remaining ingredients and whirl until dough holds together. It will be sticky. Turn onto floured board and knead a few times. Form into a sausage shape and cut in thirds. Flatten with the hands to a circle. Brush tops with melted butter and sprinkle with sugar. Cut each circle into fourths and put on ungreased cookie sheet. Bake at 425 degrees for 10 to 12 minutes, or until nicely browned. This recipe divides nicely if you don't want so many scones.

Sequim (pronounced Sqwim) receives the lowest rainfall west of the Cascades and north of San Diego, averaging 14 to 16 inches per year. Very near the Groveland Cottage is the longest sand spit (Dungeness Spit) in this country. Sequim also boasts a manned lighthouse, one of only two in the U.S. Over 350 species of birds are spotted in this area year round.

Angel Biscuits

1 tsp. DRY YEAST	**1/2 tsp. BAKING SODA**
3 Tbsp. WARM WATER	**1/2 tsp. SALT**
2 1/2 cups FLOUR	**1/2 cup BUTTER**
2 Tbsp. SUGAR	**3/4 cup BUTTERMILK,**
2 1/2 tsp. BAKING POWDER	**(approx.)**

In a 1 cup measure, dissolve yeast in water. In a large bowl, stir together flour, sugar, baking powder, soda and salt. Cut in butter until it is fine. Stir in yeast mixture and enough of the buttermilk to make a fairly soft dough. Turn out on a pastry cloth; knead a few times to smooth dough. Roll dough to 1/2 inch thickness, and cut out with a round, floured 2 inch cutter. Place a few inches apart on a greased cookie sheet. Bake in a preheated 400 degree oven until golden brown (15-18 minutes) and serve hot. Makes 12 biscuits.

Whole Wheat-Oatmeal Molasses Bread

Orcas Hotel — Orcas

1 cup OLD-FASHIONED
   ROLLED OATS
2 cups HOT COFFEE
2 tsp. BUTTER
1/2 cup MOLASSES
1 tsp SALT

1 Tbsp. DRY YEAST
1/2 cup WARM WATER
1 pinch SUGAR
2 1/2 cups WHITE FLOUR
2 1/2 cups WHOLE WHEAT
   FLOUR

Combine first five ingredients in a large mixing bowl. Let stand for 1/2 hour, stirring twice during that time. Dissolve yeast and sugar in water using a fork. Let stand for 5 minutes, or until slightly foamy. Combine flour with all other ingredients in a large mixer bowl. With the hook on #1 for 3 to 5 minutes, add more flour if dough is too sticky. Knead 3 to 5 minutes more. When finished, dough will be slightly sticky to touch. Shape dough into a ball. Place in lightly greased bowl covered with plastic wrap. Place in a warm spot to rise for 30 to 60 minutes, until twice its original size. Punch down and knead for 1 minute. Divide into two equal parts, shaping each into loaves. Score each loaf diagonally. Place each in a lightly greased bread pan. Place in warm spot again to rise to double size. Lightly brush with egg wash for a gloss finish (using 1 egg yolk with 1 Tbsp. water). Sprinkle with rolled oats. Bake in a preheated oven at 375 degrees for 35 to 45 minutes, until a hollow sound is heard when loaves are gently tapped. For a softer bread, add 2 Tbsp. yeast. Many of our senior guests have commented that this is the richest whole wheat bread they have ever eaten!

> *The Orcas Hotel is on the National Register of Historic Places. Hauntingly beautiful Orcas Island is the largest of the 172 islands in the San Juan group. Evergreen Madrona trees, with their distinct red bark, along with old growth fir, hemlock, cedar and alder all add beauty to this pristine land. The hotel welcomed its first guest in 1904, and today is still surrounded by an English country garden abundant with flowers and herbs.*

Northwest Fair Scones

2 cups FLOUR
3 Tbsp. BROWN SUGAR
2 tsp. BAKING POWDER
1/2 tsp. BAKING SODA
1/2 tsp. SALT
1/4 cup BUTTER or MARGARINE
1 ctn. (8 oz.) DAIRY SOUR CREAM
1 EGG YOLK, beaten
1 EGG WHITE, slightly beaten
JAM, or JELLY

In a large mixing bowl, stir together the flour, brown sugar, baking powder, baking soda and salt. Using a pastry blender, cut in butter till mixture resembles coarse crumbs. Make a well in center. In a small mixing bowl, stir together sour cream and egg yolk; add all at once to flour mixture. With a fork, stir till combined (mixture may seem dry). Turn dough onto a lightly floured surface. Quickly knead dough by gently folding and pressing for 10-12 strokes, or until nearly smooth. Pat or lightly roll dough into a 7-inch circle. Cut into 12 wedges. Arrange wedges on an ungreased baking sheet about 1 inch apart. Brush with egg white. Bake in 400 degree oven for 10-12 minutes until lightly brown. Cool on a wire rack for 10 minutes. While warm, split with fork and spread with butter and your choice of jam or jelly. Serve warm. Makes 12 scones.

Since 1915, scones have been a signature item at fairs and festivals throughout the Pacific Northwest. People stand in long lines just to savor these piping hot scones. In 1991, over 30,000 scones a day were served at the Puyallup fair. Now, here is your opportunity to enjoy them in your home!

Raisin Gem-Cakes

Opal Watson — Everett

1 1/2 cups SEEDLESS RAISINS
1/2 cup NUTS
1 Tbsp. GRATED ORANGE RIND
1/2 cup SHORTENING
1 cup SUGAR
2 EGGS, slightly beaten

2 cups FLOUR, sifted
1/2 tsp. SALT
1 cup BUTTERMILK
1 tsp. VANILLA
1 tsp. BAKING SODA

Glaze:
  1/4 cup SUGAR
  3 Tbsp. ORANGE JUICE
  (let stand 30 minutes)

Chop or grind raisins and nuts together, and add orange rind, and set aside. Cream shortening and sugar, beating until light and fluffy. Add eggs. In a separate bowl, mix together flour and salt. To the buttermilk, add vanilla and soda. Add flour and liquid alternately to the creamed mixture, stirring well after each addition. Fold in raisin mixture. Fill greased and floured muffin tins 2/3 full. Bake in 350 degree oven until they test done, about 20-30 minutes. Cool 5 minutes, take from pan and dip tops in glaze.

"Best Ever" Muffins

Brittany Walker — Everett

1 3/4 cup FLOUR, sifted
1/4 cup SUGAR
2 1/2 tsp. BAKING POWDER
3/4 tsp. SALT

1 EGG, well beaten
3/4 cup MILK
1/3 cup OIL or MELTED
  SHORTENING

Sift flour, sugar, baking powder and salt into bowl; make well in center. Combine the egg, milk and oil, and add all at once to dry ingredients. Stir quickly, just until dry ingredients are moistened. Fill greased muffin pans 2/3 full, and bake in 400 degree oven for 25 minutes. Give muffins a sparkling coating by dipping the tops in melted butter, then in granulated sugar while they are still warm. If you prefer blueberry muffins, prepare batter as above and add one cup fresh, or well-drained, thawed, frozen blueberries tossed with 2 Tbsp. sugar. Makes 12.

Coconut-Date-Walnut Scones

The James House Bed & Breakfast — Port Townsend

4 1/2 cups FLOUR
1/2 cup SUGAR
3 Tbsp. BAKING POWDER
2 1/2 tsp. SALT
1 cup COCONUT
1 cup CHOPPED DATES
1 cup CHOPPED WALNUTS
1 stick BUTTER
3 EGGS, beaten
1 1/4 cup MILK

Stir the first four ingredients thoroughly. Stir in the coconut, dates and walnuts. Cut in the butter until the mixture resembles coarse crumbs. Add eggs and milk and stir until dough clings together. Knead gently 12 to 15 times on a lightly floured board. Cut dough in fourths and form a patted down square from each part, about 1/2 inch thick. Cut each square diagonally twice to form four triangles. These triangles can be placed on a sheet and frozen until ready to bake. Thaw to room temperature prior to baking. Place triangles on ungreased sheet and bake at 375 degrees until golden brown, 12 to 15 minutes.

A grand Victorian mansion built by Francis James in 1889, the James House was to become the first bed and breakfast guest house in the Northwest. It is listed on the National Register of Historic Places and reflects Mr. James' love of fine woods. A short walk takes you to down- town Port Townsend, or to miles of beaches, delightful parks, or the uptown district (which was originally established to provide ladies more sedate shopping than the bawdy waterfront.)

Hot Cross Buns

The Shelburne Inn — Seaview

Sugar glaze:
1/4 cup SUGAR
5 Tbsp. MILK

Dissolve sugar in milk over low heat. Raise the heat and boil rapidly for 2 minutes. Set aside.

Buns:

8 cups all-purpose FLOUR	**1 tsp. GROUND CINNAMON**
1/2 cup plus 2 tsp. SUGAR	**1 tsp. NUTMEG, grated**
2 Tbsp. DRY YEAST	**1/2 cup BUTTER, softened**
1 1/2 cup WARM MILK	**2 EGGS, lightly beaten**
1 cup WARM WATER	**2/3 cup CURRANTS**
2 tsp. SALT	**2/3 cup DARK RAISINS**
1 tsp. ALLSPICE	**2/3 cup LIGHT RAISINS**

Mix 2 cups flour, 2 tsp. sugar, yeast, the warm milk and the warm water. Cover the bowl and set aside for 20 minutes in a warm place. Mix the remaining flour with the salt, spices and remaining sugar. Add the dry ingredients, the softened butter, beaten eggs, currants and raisins to the yeast batter. Mix it well to form a soft dough, adding extra flour if the dough is too sticky to handle. Turn the dough onto a lightly floured surface and knead it until it's smooth—that'll take about 10 minutes by hand or 2-3 minutes with a mixer and a dough hook. Shape the dough into a ball and place it in an oiled bowl. Cover and let rise in a warm place until it's doubled in bulk—this will take about an hour. Now turn it out onto a lightly floured surface, punch it down and knead for about 2 minutes. Divide the dough into 24 pieces and shape them into buns. Next place them on greased baking sheets. Cover and let rise for about 30 minutes in a warm place until they've doubled in size.

For the cross:
1/2 cup FLOUR
2-4 Tbsp. WATER

Just before putting the buns into the oven, make a cross on the top of each using a pastry tube fitted with a small opening and filled with a paste (the consistency of a thin frosting) made by mixing flour and water. Bake in a 375 degree oven for about 15-20 minutes. Transfer to a rack and brush with the sugar glaze immediately.

It's a Chocolate Pizza!

A picture-perfect candy for the Holidays.

1 pkg. (12 oz.) CHOCOLATE CHIPS
1 lb. WHITE ALMOND BARK
2 cups miniature MARSHMALLOWS
1 cup RICE KRISPIES®
1 cup PEANUTS
1 jar (6 oz.) MARASCHINO CHERRIES, cut in half
3 Tbsp GREEN MARASCHINO CHERRIES, cut in quarters
1/3 cup COCONUT
1 tsp. OIL

Melt chocolate chips with 14 ounces of the almond bark in large saucepan over low heat, stirring until smooth. Remove from heat and stir in marshmallows, cereal and peanuts. Pour onto greased 12-inch pizza pan and top with cherries. Sprinkle with the coconut. Melt remaining 2 ounces almond bark with oil over low heat, strring until smooth. Drizzle over coconut and chill until firm. Store at room temperature. Serves 16-24.

Grand Marnier Soufflé

Canlis Restaurant — Seattle

Soufflé mixture:
  18 med. EGGS, whites and yolks separated

Whip 2 cups of egg whites with 1 1/2 cups sugar, and a pinch of cream of tartar just until stiff. Set aside.

Cream sauce:
  2 cups WHIPPING CREAM
  2 Tbsp. FLOUR
  3 BUTTER PATS
  1/8 tsp. LEMON JUICE
  SALT and PEPPER to taste

Blend together and set aside (keep at room temperature).

Egg mixture:
  12 EGG YOLKS
  6 oz. GRAND MARNIER
  6 Tbsp. CREAM SAUCE
  1/2 tsp. grated ORANGE ZEST

Blend egg mixture in a separate bowl. Add the stiff egg whites by folding with a spatula (do not use whip) until well blended and lumps are gone. Pour mixture into eight souffle bowls which have been butter coated on the inner sides (do not coat bottoms), then coat with granulated sugar. Level the mixture with a spatula to the top of the bowls, then score around the inner edge of the bowl. Bake at 350 degrees for 25-30 minutes, until done. It should rise above the bowl about 2-3 inches. Sprinkle top with powdered sugar. When serving, split center with a spoon and pour in *Anglais Sauce.* Garnish with fresh whole raspberries.

Anglais Sauce

2 med. EGGS, whole   **3 cups HEAVY CREAM**
2 EGG YOLKS   **(room temp.)**
1 cup POWDERED SUGAR   **3 oz. GRAND MARNIER**
1 tsp. VANILLA EXTRACT

Mix eggs, sugar and vanilla together. Add cream. Cook over medium heat until thickened. Skim the foam off the top as it cooks. When done stir in the Grand Marnier. Keep warm.

Pear Ice in a Blackberry Puddle

Graham Kerr — Seattle

1 1/2 lbs. (2 -3) BARTLETT or COMICE PEARS
5 quarter-size slices unpeeled, fresh GINGERROOT
1 cup WATER
2/3 cup GRANULATED SUGAR
6 fresh MINT LEAVES, torn into small pieces and bruised
1 Tbsp. freshly squeezed LEMON JUICE
1 tsp. loosely packed GINGERROOT, fresh, finely chopped
1 lb. BLACKBERRIES, fresh or thawed frozen

Garnish:
5 large fresh MINT LEAVES
1 1/2 fresh PEARS

Peel the pears, keeping the flesh and peels separate. Sub-merge the pears in a bowl of water with a squeeze of lemon juice to keep the flesh from browning. Quar-ter the pears, slice out the seeds and place them back in the acidulated wa-ter. You should have approximately 1 pound of pear flesh. Put the pear trim-mings, pits and peels in a saucepan.

Add the quarter-size slices of ginger, water, sugar and mint to the pear peels and simmer over medium heat, crushing the fruit and spices with a wooden spoon or potato masher to squeeze out all of their flavor. Pour through a fine mesh sieve into a small bowl, pressing gently on the residue, without pushing any solids through. Return the liquid to saucepan, bring to a boiL and reduce to 2/3 cup—about 10 minutes. Remove from the heat and let cool.

Drain the pears, place in food processor and add the lemon juice and chopped ginger. Pulse to a semi-smooth purée—about

(Continued on next page . . .)

(Continued from previous page)

30 seconds. You want to be careful to retain some of the pears' texture for the final dish.

Pour the blackberries into a small, fine sieve and push the berries through into a bowl. You should have 1 cup of blackberry purée. Stir in the pear purée and mix well. Transfer 4 tablespoons of the mixed purées to a small bowl and set aside. Whisk the pear reduction into the pear-blackberry purée.

Ready your ice-cream maker according to the manufacturer's directions. Pour in the pear-blackberry purée and freeze until solid.

To serve: Prepare the garnish by cutting the pears into quarters. Place each pear slice lengthwise on a cutting board and cut small layers, almost to the end of the pear but not quite. Now spread the layers like a fan. Place a large mint leaf on the small dessert plate and cover the stem end with four small scoops of the ice. Dollop the reserved blackberry-pear purée to one side and place the pear garnish on top of the "puddle".

Yields 5 cups. Serves 6, generously.

Copyright © 1993 by the Treena and Graham Kerr Corporation. Reproduced with permission from G. P. Putnam's Sons.

Granny's Apricot Pudding

Jimmie Holeman — Everett

1 pkg. DRIED APRICOTS
3/4 cup SUGAR
pinch SALT
3 Tbsp. FLOUR
3 EGGS, separated
1 tsp. BUTTER
2 cups MILK
1 tsp. VANILLA
1 pkg. VANILLA WAFERS

Cook the dried apricots in very little water, then grind or sieve. Cook together until thickened; sugar, salt, flour, egg yolks, butter, milk and vanilla. Beat egg whites and fold into cooled custard. Set aside. Roll vanilla wafers into crumbs. In serving dish, alternate layers of wafers, custard and apricots. Top with wafer crumbs and serve chilled with whipped cream.

Brownies for Everyone

1/2 cup MARGARINE
1 cup SUGAR
4 EGGS
1 can (1 lb.) CHOCOLATE SYRUP
1/2 tsp. BAKING POWDER

1/2 cup WALNUTS, chopped
1/4 tsp. SALT
1 tsp. VANILLA
1 cup plus 1 Tbsp. FLOUR,
    sifted

Beat margarine with sugar until light and fluffy. Beat in eggs, two at a time, and vanilla. Mix well. Stir in syrup; sift flour, baking powder and salt. Stir into mixture and add nuts. Pour into a well greased jelly roll pan, and spread evenly. Bake at 350 degrees for 20-25 minutes. Remove pan to rack and cool.

Frosting:
6 Tbsp. MARGARINE
6 Tbsp. MILK
1 cup SUGAR

1/2 cup SEMI-SWEET
    CHOCOLATE CHIPS
1 tsp. VANILLA

Combine margarine, milk and sugar in saucepan and stir to mix. Bring to a boil for 30 seconds. Add chocolate chips, stirring until mixture thickens slightly and cool. Stir in vanilla, then spread over cooled brownies. Cut into bars. Makes 5 dozen.

Prize-Winning
Wild Blackberry Pie

Sister Mary Thorne, Church of the Assumption — Bellingham

Crust:
   2 cups FLOUR
   2/3 cup SHORTENING
   1 tsp. SALT

Filling:
   4 cups WILD BLACKBERRIES
   3/4 cup SUGAR
   1 tsp. CINNAMON
   1/4 cup FLOUR
   NUTMEG to taste (optional)

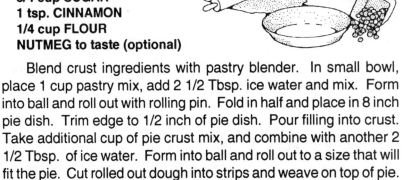

Blend crust ingredients with pastry blender. In small bowl, place 1 cup pastry mix, add 2 1/2 Tbsp. ice water and mix. Form into ball and roll out with rolling pin. Fold in half and place in 8 inch pie dish. Trim edge to 1/2 inch of pie dish. Pour filling into crust. Take additional cup of pie crust mix, and combine with another 2 1/2 Tbsp. of ice water. Form into ball and roll out to a size that will fit the pie. Cut rolled out dough into strips and weave on top of pie. Trim the edge to 1/2 inch over pie dish. Fold under with bottom crust. Using thumb and index fingers, make a fluted edge. Bake at 375 degrees for one hour. Let cool for 2 or 3 hours and enjoy! This pie is tart. If you like sweeter pie, use 1 cup of sugar. Wild blackberries are found in the first part of July in cleared areas.

As a young girl, Sister Mary and her family lived in Sequim, where they picked many gallons of wild blackberries near their home. Her pie won blue ribbon prizes at the Clallam County Fair, the Northwest Washington Fair and the Yakima State Fair, in the same year.

Peanut Butter Fudge Pie

Tracey Walker — Bellingham

1 pkg. (8 oz.) CREAM CHEESE
1/2 cup PEANUT BUTTER
1 cup POWDERED SUGAR, sifted
2 Tbsp. MILK
1 tsp. VANILLA
4 oz. FROZEN DESSERT TOPPING, thawed
1 GRAHAM CRACKER PIE SHELL
3/4 cup FUDGE ICE CREAM TOPPING

Soften cream cheese, add peanut butter and beat with mixer until combined. Add sugar, milk and vanilla and beat until combined. Fold in dessert topping. Spoon half the cream cheese mixture in pie shell, and spread with 1/2 cup fudge topping. Place remaining mixture in crust; cover and freeze at least 6 hours. Let pie stand at room temperature 15 minutes before serving. Drizzle with topping and sprinkle with chopped peanuts.

Apricot Pie a la Holmes

James Walker, Prof. of Physics, Wash. State University — Pullman

1 lb. DRIED APRICOTS
6 EGGS, separated
1 UNBAKED PIE SHELL

SUGAR, to taste
VANILLA, to taste

The apricots are cooked, and pressed through a sieve. The egg whites are whipped quite stiff, and mixed with the sweetened apricot mash. The mixture is then baked in pie shell at 350 degrees about 20 minutes. The yolks are whipped with sugar and vanilla and are served cold over the hot pie.

Langley, the village by the sea, is at the southern tip of Whidbey Island, second largest island in the United States. Every year, Langley hosts a Mystery Weekend. Participants come from near and far to pick up clues at local business firms, in an attempt to solve a fictional murder. Many participants, as well as Prof. Walker, dress for the occasion in Sherlock Holmes attire.

Sour Cream King Apple Pie

Albatross Bed & Breakfast — Anacortes

1 UNBAKED PIE SHELL	1 cup LIGHT SOUR CREAM
1 EGG, separated	1 1/4 tsp. VANILLA
2/3 cup SUGAR	4 1/2 cups KING APPLES,
2 Tbsp. FLOUR	finely chopped
dash SALT	

Beat egg white until frothy and brush on the inside of the pie shell. Bake in 375 degree oven for 8 minutes. Stir together the sugar, flour and salt. Combine with sour cream, egg yolk and vanilla. Stir in apples, and spoon into pie shell. Squeeze handfuls of **Crumble Topping** onto pie. Bake at 375 degrees for 65 minutes.

Crumble Topping

6 Tbsp. BUTTER	1/4 tsp. GINGER
1/2 cup BROWN SUGAR	1/2 cup WALNUTS, chopped
3/4 tsp. CINNAMON	

Mix brown sugar, cinnamon and ginger together. Cut butter in until crumbly and then stir in walnuts.

A great adventure awaits those who ferry from Anacortes, the home of famed ballad-singer, Burl Ives. The adventure takes visitors through the forested San Juan Islands, home to many orca whales, bald eagles, seals, porpoises, otters, waterfowl, black-tailed deer and 10,000 people.

Peanut Butter Pie

Collector's Choice Restaurant — Snohomish

4 oz. SOFT BUTTER
1 cup POWDERED SUGAR
1/2 cup CREAMY PEANUT BUTTER
2 EGGS
2 cups WHIPPED TOPPING
1 baked 8-9 inch PIE CRUST

Topping:
  2 oz. CHOCOLATE CHIPS
  2 to 2 1/2 Tbsp. WHIPPING CREAM

In a mixing bowl, whip butter until fluffy and light in color. Add sugar and whip again until fluffy. Add peanut butter to butter/sugar mixture and whip. Add one egg and whip 2 minutes. Scrape down sides of bowl, add second egg and whip another 2 minutes. Again, scrape sides of bowl. Fold in topping until smooth but do not beat or over-mix. Pour into pie shell, mounding toward the center. For topping; over hot water, melt chocolate chips and whipping cream. Stir to combine, then cool. Drizzle over pie with a spoon and chill. Yields one, 8-9 inch tin of fabulous dessert.

This dessert is "to die for". Snohomish, on the Snohomish River, is the "Antique Capital of the Northwest". This fine restaurant occupies the main level of the largest antique mall in the Pacific Northwest.

Bread Pudding

Opal Watson — Everett

2 cups BREAD, cubed
1/2 cup ALL BRAN CEREAL
1/2 cup CHOCOLATE CHIPS
3 EGGS, beaten

1/2 cup SUGAR
1/4 tsp. SALT
3 cups MILK
1 tsp. VANILLA

Place bread cubes and cereal in a buttered oblong baking dish. Sprinkle with half of chocolate chips. Combine beaten eggs, sugar, salt, milk and vanilla. Pour over bread and top with remaining chocolate chips. Place baking dish in pan of hot water, and bake one hour at 325 degrees.

Superb Strawberry Pie

Pastry:
- 1 heaping cup FLOUR
- 1/2 cup MARGARINE
- 3 1/2 Tbsp. POWDERED SUGAR

Filling:
- 1 cup SUGAR
- 3 Tbsp. plus 2 tsp. CORNSTARCH
- 1 1/2 cups WATER
- 3 Tbsp. WHITE CORN SYRUP
- 4 Tbsp. STRAWBERRY GELATIN POWDER
- 2 drops RED FOOD COLORING
- 1 qt. FRESH STRAWBERRIES

Cut margarine into flour and powdered sugar. Press into a 9 inch pie pan and bake at 350 degrees for 20 minutes, then cool. Combine in a saucepan sugar and cornstarch adding water and corn syrup. Bring to a boil and cook 6 minutes, stirring constantly. Remove from heat and add dry jello and red food coloring and set aside to cool. Clean and slice the strawberries and stir into the cooled mixture. Pour into pie crust and allow to set. This is also very good when made with fresh raspberries and raspberry gelatin.

Banana Split Dessert

- 1 cup FLOUR, sifted
- 1/2 cup PECANS, chopped
- 1/4 cup BROWN SUGAR
- 1/4 cup MARGARINE, melted
- 2 to 3 BANANAS
- 1/2 gal. NEAPOLITAN ICE CREAM
- 1 cup CHOCOLATE CHIPS
- 1/2 cup BUTTER
- 2 cups POWDERED SUGAR
- 1 1/2 cups EVAPORATED MILK
- 1 tsp. VANILLA
- WHIPPED CREAM for garnish
- 1 cup WALNUTS, chopped

Mix flour, pecans, brown sugar and melted margarine. Spread evenly in 11 x 15 inch foil-lined pan. Bake at 350 degrees for 10-20 minutes. Stir several times until light brown in color. In another 11 x 15 inch pan, cover bottom with crumbs you just made, saving 1 cup for topping. Slice bananas and layer over crumbs. Slice ice cream in 1/2 inch layers, and place on top of bananas. Freeze until firm. Melt chips and butter, add powdered sugar and milk. Cook mixture until thick and smooth, stirring constantly. Remove from heat and add vanilla and cool. Pour over ice cream and re-freeze. Add whipped cream and nuts when serving. Serves 25.

Mile-High Apple Pie

Washington Apple Commission — Wenatchee

Pastry:
- **2 1/4 cups FLOUR, unsifted**
- **1/2 tsp. SALT**
- **1/2 cup VEGETABLE SHORTENING**
- **5 Tbsp. BUTTER, chilled**
- **4-5 Tbsp. COLD WATER**

Apple Filling:
- **12 GRANNY SMITH APPLES, peeled, cored, thinly sliced**
- **1 cup SUGAR**
- **2 tsp. GROUND CINNAMON**
- **1/2 tsp. GROUND NUTMEG**
- **1 tsp. VANILLA EXTRACT**

Butter-Pecan crumb:
- **1 cup FLOUR, unsifted**
- **1/3 cup SUGAR**
- **1/4 tsp. SALT**
- **1/2 cup (1 stick) BUTTER, softened**
- **1/2 cup PECANS, chopped**

 Prepare pastry: In large bowl, combine flour and salt. Cut vegetable shortening and butter into flour mixture until coarsely blended. Gradually add water, stirring gently, until dough binds when pressed between fingers. Form dough into two balls, one slightly larger than the other, wrap and refrigerate.

Make Apple Filling: In large pot over medium-low heat, cover and cook apple slices, stirring occasionally, until barely tender (about 10 minutes). Drain apple slices completely. Transfer to large bowl, add sugar, cinnamon, nutmeg and vanilla. Stir gently to blend. Set aside.

Prepare Butter-Pecan Crumb: In medium-sized bowl, combine flour, sugar and salt. Cut butter into flour mixture until coarsely blended. Add pecans and rub mixture briefly between fingers to form crumbs. Heat oven to 400 degrees. Roll out smaller piece of dough to an 11-inch round; transfer to 9-inch pie plate and line bottom and sides. Fill pie bottom with apple filling, mounding in center. Roll out larger piece of dough to a 12-inch round and transfer to top of pie, covering filling, trim and pinch edges of bottom and top crusts. Brush top crust lightly with water and gently press crumb topping to crust. Make several slits in top crust of pie to vent steam; bake 45-50 minutes until crust is golden brown. Cool at least 25 minutes, sift confectioners' sugar over top and serve. Serves 12.

Rhubarb Delight

Crust:
  1 cup FLOUR
  2 Tbsp. WHITE SUGAR
  1/2 cup BUTTER or MARGARINE

  Mix until crumbly and pat into 8 x 11 pan.
  Bake at 325 degrees, 10 minutes.

Filling:
  4 cups RHUBARB, diced
  2 cups SUGAR
  3/4 cup MILK
  4 Tbsp. FLOUR
  3 EGG YOLKS, beaten

  Mix and pour over baked crust.
  Bake at 325 degrees for 45 minutes.

Meringue:
  3 EGG WHITES
  1/4 tsp. CREAM OF TARTAR
  5 Tbsp. SUGAR

  Spread meringue on baked filling, and bake at 400 degrees, 8-10 minutes.

Rhubarb makes an interesting addition to applesauce for taste and color. Rhubarb and strawberries are another popular combination, either stewed or in pie. Try adding strained juice from stewed rhubarb to add color and flavor to fruit punch!

Baked Rhubarb

4 cups RHUBARB, sliced
1 cup SUGAR
2 Tbsp. WATER or SHERRY
1/4 tsp. NUTMEG
1/2 tsp. LEMON PEEL, grated

  Mix thoroughly and turn into buttered 2-quart baking dish. Cover and bake at 350 degrees for 40-45 minutes, until tender. Rhubarb keeps it color and shape best when baked. Serves 6.

Rhubarb Cake

1/2 cup BUTTER or MARGARINE
1 1/2 cups BROWN SUGAR
1/2 pt. SOUR CREAM
2 cups FLOUR
1 tsp. BAKING SODA

1/2 tsp. SALT
1 tsp. VANILLA
1 cup RHUBARB, cut-up
   into 1/2 inch pieces

Cream together butter and sugar and add sour cream. Sift together flour, soda, and salt. Add vanilla and rhubarb and mix all ingredients together. Spread into greased 9 x 13 pan, and sprinkle with topping.

Topping:
   3/4 cup BROWN SUGAR
   1 tsp. CINNAMON
   2 Tbsp. BUTTER

Sprinkle over top, and bake at 350 degrees for 40 minutes.

Did you know that you can clean discolored aluminum pots by boiling rhubarb in them?

Dad Horton's Rhubarb Dessert

Joyce Fowler — Puyallup

4 cups RHUBARB, chopped
1 cup SUGAR
1/2 stick BUTTER, melted

Spread chopped rhubarb in a 9 x 9 pan, sprinkle sugar over it and pour melted butter over all.

Cake Batter:
   1 cup SUGAR
   1/2 cup SHORTENING
   1 EGG
   1/2 cup MILK

1 cup FLOUR
1 tsp. BAKING POWDER
1 tsp. VANILLA
1/2 tsp. SALT

Mix batter and spread over rhubarb mixture. Bake at 350 degrees for 45 minutes or until browned to your favor.

Cranberry Sorbet

Congressman Al Swift, U. S. House of Representatives

2 pkgs. (12 oz. ea.) FRESH CRANBERRIES
4 FRESH ORANGES, peeled, quartered or sectioned
2 pkgs. (12 oz. ea.) FROZEN RASPBERRIES, with sugar
2 cups SUGAR

Clean cranberries in water, discarding stems and poor, soft berries. Put in a food processor bowl with the orange sections and blend thoroughly. Force the mixture through a sieve to eliminate seeds. Process the raspberries and sieve the seeds. Mix the two together, add sugar to taste and process. In a shallow dish, freeze the mixture until nearly solid. (If it should freeze, let thaw briefly before proceeding.) Process the semi-frozen mixture to lighten and increase smoothness. Return mixture to dish, and re-freeze. Shortly before serving, remove from freezer, but remember the sorbet melts very quickly. Using raspberries without sugar will require more sugar than called for. If you prefer, use fewer raspberries to enhance the cranberry taste.

"Life is just a bowl of cherries," but not in Washington. Here it's more like 93,000 tons a year! That's because this state leads the nation in cherry production. About half the crop is processed into maraschinos, frozen, or used for juice and in ice cream.

Mystery Cherry Cobbler

1 cup FLOUR
1 cup SUGAR
2 tsp. BAKING POWDER
2/3 cup MILK

1 tsp. VANILLA
1 can (16 oz.) SOUR
 CHERRIES, pitted
2/3 cup SUGAR, or to taste

Grease a 1 1/2 quart casserole. Preheat oven to 350 degrees. Combine dry ingredients in mixing bowl and slowly add milk. Add vanilla. Pour batter into casserole. Drain juice from cherries, put into a saucepan and add sugar to taste. Heat only until sugar dissolves. Place cherries in the heated juice and pour gently over batter. Bake 25 to 35 minutes. Dough rises to the top while baking. Serve warm, with ice cream or half & half.

Pumpkin Crunch

1 lg. can PUMPKIN
1 1/2 cups SUGAR
5 EGGS, beaten
1 (13 oz. can) EVAPORATED MILK
2 tsp. PUMPKIN PIE SPICE
1 box WHITE SOUR CREAM CAKE MIX
1 cup BUTTER, melted
3/4 cup NUTS, chopped

Mix pumpkin, sugar, beaten eggs, milk and spice together. Place in prepared 9 x 13 baking dish, and sprinkle the dry cake mix and nuts over, pouring the melted butter over all. Bake at 325 degrees, 50 to 55 minutes.

Cookie Sheet Apple Pie

2 1/2 cups FLOUR
1 cup SHORTENING
1 1/2 tsp. SALT
2 EGG YOLKS, beaten, plus enough milk to make 2/3 cup

Cut flour, shortening and salt until crumbly, add egg and milk mixture. Mix until it forms a ball. Divide in half. Roll out each half into a 10 x 15 rectangle. Place one in greased and floured 10 x 15 x 2 jelly-roll pan. Set aside.

Filling:
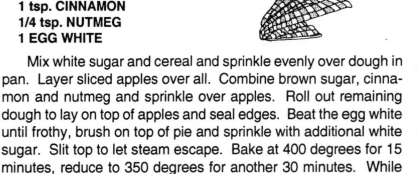
　　1 cup SUGAR
　　1 cup RAISIN BRAN, crushed
　　6 to 8 cups APPLES, sliced
　　1/2 cup BROWN SUGAR
　　1 tsp. CINNAMON
　　1/4 tsp. NUTMEG
　　1 EGG WHITE

Mix white sugar and cereal and sprinkle evenly over dough in pan. Layer sliced apples over all. Combine brown sugar, cinnamon and nutmeg and sprinkle over apples. Roll out remaining dough to lay on top of apples and seal edges. Beat the egg white until frothy, brush on top of pie and sprinkle with additional white sugar. Slit top to let steam escape. Bake at 400 degrees for 15 minutes, reduce to 350 degrees for another 30 minutes. While warm from oven, drizzle with powdered sugar frosting. Serves 20.

Dutch Apple Pie

Jennifer Knudson — Mukilteo

9-inch unbaked PIE SHELL
4 cups APPLES (Johnathan, Winesap, or MacIntosh apples only)
1/8 tsp. CINNAMON
1 3/4 cups GRANULATED SUGAR
1/4 cup FLOUR
1/2 tsp. SALT
3 Tbsp. MILK
6 Tbsp. COFFEE CREAM

Peel, core and cut apples into 3/4 inch cubes. Place in pie shell and spread evenly. Sprinkle cinnamon over apples. Mix sugar, flour and salt together; add milk and cream and beat 8-10 minutes at medium speed. Pour evenly over all apples. Bake in a 375 degree oven for 60-75 minutes. Serve warm.

"This is absolutely the best apple pie ever made. This generous fruit filling should be slightly precooked to reduce the juice that can soften the pastry crust."

Pumpkin Squares

36 GINGER SNAP COOKIES
1/2 gal. VANILLA ICE CREAM
1 can (1 lb.) PUMPKIN
1 cup SUGAR

1 tsp. SALT
1 tsp. GINGER
1/2 tsp. NUTMEG

Crush cookies and cover bottom of 9 x 13 pan with half the cookies, and set aside. Soften ice cream and set aside. In a chilled bowl, mix remaining ingredients, stirring well. Combine with ice cream. Pour over crushed cookies and cover ice cream mixture with balance of cookies. Freeze for at least 5 hours.

Cran-Apple Bread Pudding

Washington Apple Commission

Bread Pudding:
- **1 lb. loaf CINNAMON-RAISIN BREAD, sliced**
- **1 qt. MILK**
- **3/4 cup LIGHT BROWN SUGAR, firmly packed**
- **2 Tbsp. LEMON ZEST**
- **1 Tbsp. VANILLA EXTRACT**
- **5 large EGGS**
- **2 ROME APPLES, cored, cubed**
- **1 cup CRANBERRIES, coarsely chopped**
- **1/2 cup WALNUTS, chopped**

Cider Sauce:
- **3 cups APPLE CIDER**
- **1 Tbsp. CORNSTARCH, dissolved in 1 Tbsp. water**
- **2 Tbsp. HALF & HALF**

Heat oven to 200 degrees. Lay bread slices on racks in oven and bake until dry, but not toasted, about 15 minutes. Remove from oven. Set aside. Increase oven temperature to 350 degrees. Grease a 10-inch tube pan. In small saucepan, combine milk, brown sugar, lemon zest, and vanilla; heat on low, stirring, until sugar dissolves. Remove from heat. In large bowl, beat eggs until frothy; slowly stir in milk mixture. Tear bread into small pieces and add to liquid mixture. Stir in apples, cranberries and walnuts until blended. Set bread pudding mixture aside 5 minutes or until bread absorbs most of liquid and softens. Spoon into prepared pan and bake 40-45 minutes. While pudding is cooling, prepare cider sauce. In saucepan, simmer cider until reduced to 1 1/2 cups. Stirring constantly, add cornstarch mixture. Bring to a boil and cook until thickened. Remove from heat and stir in half & half. Turn pudding out onto plate and serve with cider sauce. Serves 12.

> *"There are as many recipes for bread pudding as there are bakers. Nearly all use generous amounts of heavy cream and butter, which, though delicious, laden the pudding with fat. In this version, we substitute milk, add lots of fruit and serve with a cornstarch-thickened sauce for a rich-tasting finish."*

Five Layer Dessert

1 cup FLOUR
1 cube BUTTER or MARGARINE
1 cup NUTS, chopped
1 pkg. (8 oz.) CREAM CHEESE, softened
1 cup POWDERED SUGAR
1 lg. container FROZEN WHIPPED TOPPING, thawed
2 sm. pkgs. INSTANT VANILLA PUDDING
3 cups MILK
1 medium can CRUSHED PINEAPPLE, drained

For the first layer, cut butter into flour until crumbly; stir in nuts and press mixture evenly in 9 x 13 baking pan. Bake at 350 degrees, 15 minutes or until browned; cool. For the second layer, combine cream cheese and powdered sugar; mix well and blend in 1 cup whipped topping. Spread over crust. For the third layer, combine pudding and milk; prepare according to package directions and spread over second layer. Spread pineapple evenly over pudding layer. For the final layer, spread pineapple with a layer of whipped topping to taste. Serve immediately or store in refrigerator. Note: If desired, recipe can be halved and placed in an 8-inch square pan.

Magic Nut Cake

3 EGGS
1 can (16 oz.) PUMPKIN
3/4 cup OIL
1/2 cup WATER
2 1/2 cups FLOUR
2 1/4 cups SUGAR
1 1/2 tsp. BAKING SODA
1 1/4 tsp. SALT
3/4 tsp. NUTMEG
3/4 tsp. CINNAMON
1 cup RAISINS
1/2 to 1 cup WALNUTS, chopped

Combine eggs, pumpkin, oil and water, and beat together. Then add the remaining ingredients. Pour into 3 medium size loaf pans. Bake at 350 degrees for 1 hour. Frost with cream cheese frosting.

Sour Cream Coffee Cake

'37 House Bed and Breakfast — Yakima

Cake:

1 cup BUTTER	1 tsp. VANILLA
2 cups SUGAR	2 cups FLOUR
2 EGGS, beaten	1 Tbsp. BAKING POWDER
2 cups SOUR CREAM	1/4 tsp. SALT

Topping:

2 cups finely chopped PECANS (or almonds)	1 Tbsp. CINNAMON
	1 cup SUGAR

Grease 10-inch bundt pan, and dust with flour. Cream butter and sugar. Add eggs, sour cream and vanilla. Fold in dry ingredients. In separate bowl, mix topping ingredients. Pour half of the batter into the bundt pan. Sprinkle 1/2 topping mixture onto batter. Add remaining batter and sprinkle remaining topping. Bake at 350 degrees for 50 minutes. Serve warm.

Aplets Candy

Jimmie Holeman — Everett

2 Tbsp. GELATIN	1 cup NUTS, chopped
1/2 cup APPLE SAUCE	1 tsp. VANILLA
3/4 cup APPLE, peeled, grated	1/2 cup POWDERED SUGAR
2 cups SUGAR	

Dissolve gelatin in apple sauce. Combine apples and sugar in large sauce pan and stir in the apple sauce mixture. Cook until thick and light brown, about 15 minutes. Add nuts and vanilla. Pour into 6 x 9 1/2 pan, let stand overnight. Cut into squares, coat pieces with powdered sugar. Makes 3-4 dozen pieces.

Aplets and Cotlets are candies that have been made commercially for 65 years in Cashmere. Cotlets are made with apricots, aplets with apples as in the recipe above.

The Ultimate Caramel Apple!

The Apple Growers of Washington State

1 cup WATER
1 cup SUGAR
1/2 cup HEAVY CREAM
6 RED or GOLDEN DELICIOUS APPLES
3 oz. WHITE CHOCOLATE,
    finely chopped
3 oz. SEMI-SWEET CHOCOLATE,
    finely chopped
1/4 cup PISTACHIOS,
    coarsely chopped
RED HOTS® or other small candy
GOLD LEAF (optional)

In a heavy bottom saucepan, combine water and sugar. Over low heat, stir mixture gently until sugar is completely dissolved. Increase heat to medium-low and cook, without stirring, until mixture is a dark amber color. Remove from heat and carefully stir in heavy cream. Mixture will bubble up and spatter a bit, but then subside. Set aside until barely warm and thickened. Insert popsicle sticks into bottom center of apples. Have at hand a piece of styrofoam, about 10-inches square, to use as a stand for apples. Cover the top of styrofoam with waxed paper to catch any caramel drippings. Dip top half of each apple into thickened caramel; stand caramel-topped apples in styrofoam, allowing caramel to run down sides; refrigerate to harden. Meanwhile, melt white chocolate in top of double boiler of gently simmering water, stir until smooth. Transfer melted chocolate to pastry bag fitted with small writing tip. Drizzle thin, random lines of chocolate over each apple. Repeat melting and drizzling with semi-sweet chocolate. Decorate each apple with pistachios, Red Hots (or other candies), and a few small pieces of gold leaf, if desired. Serve—or refrigerate to serve later. Serves 6.

"Homemade caramel is a luscious culinary invention, well worth the effort".

Banana-Nut Cake

3/4 cup SHORTENING
1 1/2 cups SUGAR
2 EGGS
3/4 cup BANANA, mashed,
   (1 large, ripe)
1 tsp. VANILLA
1 3/4 cups FLOUR

1 tsp. BAKING SODA
1 tsp. BAKING POWDER
1/2 tsp. SALT
2/3 cup BUTTERMILK or
   SOUR MILK
1/2 cup chopped WALNUTS
   or PECANS

In a large mixer bowl, beat shortening and sugar on high speed until light and fluffy. Add eggs, beat 2 minutes at medium speed. Add mashed banana and vanilla; beat 2 minutes more. In another small bowl, stir together flour, baking soda, baking powder and salt; add to creamed mixture alternately with buttermilk, beating well after each addition. Stir in the chopped nuts. Pour batter into two greased and floured 9-inch round cake pans. Bake at 375 degrees for 25 minutes, or till toothpick comes out clean off center. Cool layers in pans 10 minutes; invert onto wire racks to cool completely. Meanwhile, prepare *Creamy Nut Filling* and *Powdered Sugar Frosting.* To assemble cake; place one cake layer on a serving plate. Spread with all of the Filling mixture. Top with second cake layer. Frost top and sides of cake with frosting. Garnish cake with whole walnuts or pecans.

Creamy Nut Filling

1/2 cup packed BROWN SUGAR
2 Tbsp. FLOUR
1/2 cup EVAPORATED MILK
2 Tbsp. BUTTER or MARGARINE

1/3 cup WALNUTS or
   PECANS, finely chopped
1/2 tsp. VANILLA
dash SALT

In a medium saucepan, stir together brown sugar and flour; stir in milk. Add butter; cook, stirring constantly, till mixture is thickened and bubbly. Remove from heat; stir in chopped nuts, vanilla, and salt. Chill 1 to 2 hours.

Powdered Sugar Frosting

1 EGG WHITE
1/2 cup SHORTENING
1/4 cup BUTTER or MARGARINE

1 tsp. VANILLA
2 cups sifted POWDERED
   SUGAR

In a medium mixer bowl beat together egg white, shortening, butter and vanilla on medium speed of mixer until well blended. Gradually add powdered sugar beating until light and fluffy.

Caramel Frosting

2 cups BROWN SUGAR
1/2 cup BUTTER
1/2 cup EVAPORATED MILK
1 1/2 tsp. VANILLA

Place sugar, butter and milk in a saucepan over medium heat, and bring to a boil, stirring constantly for 5 minutes. Remove from heat, add vanilla, and beat until desired spreading consistency. This is delicious on a chocolate cake.

Fudge Sundae Topping

1/2 cup COCOA
3/4 cup SUGAR
2/3 cup EVAPORATED MILK
1/3 cup CORN SYRUP
1/3 cup MARGARINE
1 tsp. VANILLA

Combine cocoa, sugar, milk and syrup and blend well. Cook over medium heat until boiling. Boil and stir 1 minute. Remove from heat and add margarine and vanilla. Excellent when drizzled on top of vanilla ice cream.

Butterscotch Glaze

1 cup SUGAR
1/2 cup BUTTERMILK
1/4 cup CORN SYRUP
1/4 cup MARGARINE
1/2 tsp. BAKING SODA
1/2 tsp. VANILLA

Place ingredients in a saucepan over medium heat. Bring to a boil, stirring constantly for 10 minutes. Pour over warm cake, especially good served on carrot cake.

Beverages

Apple Cooler

The Apple Growers of Washington State

3 GOLDEN DELICIOUS APPLES,
   peeled, cored, finely chopped
1/2 cup WATER

2 Tbsp. LEMON JUICE
2 cups ROSÉ WINE
2 cups CLUB SODA

In saucepan, simmer apples, water and lemon juice 20 minutes or until mixture has consistency of applesauce; purée in blender or food processor. Cool to room temperature. To serve, combine equal parts of apple purée, wine and soda in six ice filled glasses.

 About 75 million, 42-pound boxes of crisp, colorful apples are produced on 160,000 Washington acres yearly.

Spiced Hot Apple Cider

Phillip Knudson — Mukilteo

1 qt. APPLE JUICE
2 3 inch WHOLE CINNAMON STICK

5 WHOLE CLOVES
10 WHOLE ALLSPICE

Mix all ingredients in large saucepan, let simmer 30 minutes. It's a great children's favorite for Halloween.

New Year's Eve Punch

1 env. RASPBERRY KOOL AID®
3/4 cup SUGAR
1/2 cup ORANGE JUICE
1/4 cup LEMON JUICE
1 can (12 oz.) PINEAPPLE JUICE

Dissolve Kool Aid and sugar in 4 cups water. Add remaining ingredients. Makes 1 1/2 quarts.

Milk Jug Punch

1 sm. STRAWBERRY GELATIN
1 pkg. STRAWBERRY KOOL AID®
1 cup SUGAR
1 can (46 oz.) PINEAPPLE JUICE
1 qt. GINGER ALE, chilled
WATER

Dissolve gelatin in 1 cup hot water with sugar and kool aid. Place pineapple juice in plastic gallon jug, add the mixture, and shake to mix. Add enough cold water to fill the jug and chill. Add ginger ale at serving time.

Holiday Berry Punch

1 pkg. (10 oz.) FROZEN STRAWBERRIES
1 can (12 oz.) FROZEN CONCENTRATED CRAN-RASPBERRY JUICE
1 can (12 oz.) FROZEN LEMONADE
1 ltr. GINGER ALE, chilled
2 ltr. SELTZER, chilled

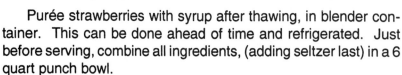

Purée strawberries with syrup after thawing, in blender container. This can be done ahead of time and refrigerated. Just before serving, combine all ingredients, (adding seltzer last) in a 6 quart punch bowl.

Citrus Punch

1 1/2 cup SUGAR
2 cup BOILING WATER
4 oz. ORANGE GELATIN
46 oz. PINEAPPLE JUICE, chilled
2 cups LEMON JUICE, chilled
32 oz. CLUB SODA
1 qt. ORANGE SHERBERT

Dissolve sugar in boiling water, add orange gelatin. Add chilled ingredients, but do not add sherbert until serving time.

Quick 'n Easy Party Drink

1 pkg. CHERRY KOOL AID®
1 pkg. RASPBERRY KOOL AID®
2 cups SUGAR
2 qts. WATER
1 can (46 oz.) UNSWEETENED PINEAPPLE JUICE
2 qt. GINGER ALE

Combine ingredients, except ginger ale, and chill. At serving time, pour into punch bowl and add ginger ale. Makes 50 punch cup servings.

Lemonade Syrup

1 tsp. LEMON RIND, grated
1 cup LEMON JUICE (4-5 LEMONS)
3/4 to 1 cup SUGAR
4 1/2 cups WATER
1 LEMON, sliced

Prepare lemon syrup: combine the rind, juice and sugar in a 4 cup container. Chill covered until ready to use. **Lemonade by the pitcher:** Combine the lemon syrup along with the 4 1/2 cups of water, and lemon slices. Stir to mix, and add ice cubes just before serving. **Lemonade by the glass:** Measure 3 Tbsp. lemon syrup (more or less according to taste) into 10 ounce glass, and add ice cubes and water, stirring to mix. **Lemon spritzer:** Put 2-3 Tbsp. of syrup in 10 oz. stemmed glass, add chilled club soda and garnish with lemon wedge.

Fireside Coffee

2 cups INSTANT SWISS MISS® COCOA MIX
2 cups DRY NONDAIRY CREAMER
1 cup INSTANT COFFEE
1 1/2 cups POWDERED SUGAR
1/2 Ttsp. CINNAMON
1/2 tsp. NUTMEG

Mix ingredients thoroughly. Store in moisture-proof container, and when ready to use, place 3 tsp. in coffee mug and add hot water.

Orange Slurpee

Gary James Knudson — Mukilteo

1/4 cup SUGAR, heaping
6 oz. ORANGE JUICE CONCENTRATE, frozen
3 cups ICE CUBES
1 cup MILK
1 cup WATER
1 tsp. VANILLA or to taste

Place all ingredients into blender container, and blend for 35 seconds. Pour into glass, and enjoy!

Soap Lake's water is alkaline, saltier than the ocean, and feels soapy. Local Indians referred to it as "healing waters." It is supposed to relieve rheumatism, skin problems and digestion.

Sunshine Drink

1 EGG
3/4 cup ORANGE JUICE
4 Tbsp. DRY MILK
2 tsp. SUGAR
4 ICE CUBES

Place all ingredients in blender, and blend at high speed.

Homemade Cocoa Mix

2 cups POWDERED MILK
1/4 cup COCOA
1 cup POWDERED SUGAR
dash SALT

Combine ingredients and store in covered container. To use, place 4 Tbsp. of mix into a cup of boiling water. Add a dash of whipped topping or vanilla. For a richer mix, add 2/3 cup powdered non-dairy creamer.

Environmental Tips

These environmentally friendly tips cost less than the toxic and hazardous household cleaners! The only supplies necessary are the usual household commodities, borax, mineral oil, scouring powder (non-chlorinated) and vegetable oil based liquid soap (Murphy's® Oil Soap).

AIR FRESHENER: Slice lemon, orange or grapferuit and simmer in pot of hot water for an hour or more.

ALL-PURPOSE HOUSE CLEANER: Combine 1 tsp. liquid soap, 1 tsp. borax, 1 qt. warm water, and 1 Tbsp. lemon juice (or vinegar).

ALUMINUM SPOT REMOVAL: Quart of hot water with 2 Tbsp. Cream of Tartar.

APPLIANCE CLEANER: Combine 1 tsp. borax, 2 Tbsp. vinegar, 1/4 tsp. liquid soap and 2 cups very hot water. Gently shake until borax has dissolved.

BLEACH: Use borax as a substitute.

BRASS POLISH: Worcestershire sauce.

CHROME POLISH: Apple cider vinegar.

COFFEE CUP STAIN REMOVAL: Moist salt.

COFFEE POT STAINS: Vinegar.

COPPER CLEANER: Lemon juice and salt.

DRAIN CLEANER: Use plunger first; then pour in 1/2 cup baking soda, followed by 1/2 cup vinegar. Close drain and wait 5 minutes. Pour in tea kettle of boiling water. Repeat as needed.

FLOOR CLEANER: (for a lasting shine, on wood, tile or linoleum); 1/8 cup vegetable based detergent, 1/2 cup white vinegar and 2 gal. warm water.

FURNITURE DUSTING (WOOD): Mix 1/2 tsp. olive oil and 1/4 cup white vinegar or lemon juice and apply to cotton cloth. Reapply as needed.

FURNITURE POLISH: Almond or linseed oil.

GREASE REMOVAL: Borax on a damp cloth.

HARDWOOD FLOORS: Scrub with solution of 1 gal. warm water and 1 qt. vinegar.

INK SPOT REMOVER: Cold water with 1 Tbsp. cream of tartar and 1 Tbsp. lemon juice.

LINOLEUM FLOOR CLEANER: 1 cup white vinegar plus 2 gal. water.

MILDEW REMOVER: Equal parts vinegar and salt.

NON-ABRASIVE CLEANSER: Combine 1/4 cup baking soda and enough vegetable based detergent to make a creamy paste.

OIL STAIN REMOVAL: White chalk rubbed into stain before laundering.

OVEN CLEANER: 2 Tbsp. liquid soap plus 2 tsp. borax mixed with warm water.

PERSPIRATION STAIN REMOVER: White vinegar plus water.

PET ODOR REMOVAL: Cider vinegar.

RUG OR CARPET CLEANER: Club soda.

SCOURING POWDER: Baking soda.

SPOT REMOVER: Club soda, lemon juice, or salt.

STAINLESS STEEL POLISH: Mineral oil.

TOILET BOWL CLEANER: Paste of borax and lemon juice, or if you prefer, pour 1 cup borax into toilet bowl, let set overnight, flush in the morning. Stains and rings are lifted out.

TUB AND TILE CLEANER: 1/4 cup baking soda plus 1/2 cup white vinegar mixed with warm water.

UPHOLSTERY SPOT REMOVAL: Club soda.

WATER MARK REMOVAL: Toothpaste.

WINE STAIN REMOVAL: Salt.

WINDOW CLEANER: Mix 1/4 cup white vinegar to 1 qt. warm water. Or, shake up 1/2 tsp. liquid soap, 3 Tbsp. vinegar and 2 cups of water in a spray bottle.

Index

Washington is the world leader in the production of the raspberry. More than 42 million pounds are produced here annually, compared to the number two producer, Hungary, at 26.4 million pounds.

About the Author

Janet Walker, mother of three and grandmother to four, resides in the Evergreen City of Everett, Washington just north of metropolitan Seattle.

For as long as she can remember, it has been her passion to cook, experiment with new recipes and collect those of others.

A native of Tulsa, Oklahoma, her parents moved to Anacortes, Washington when she was only eight years old. There she later met and married her husband, Ivan.

Her first effort as an author of a cook book was the highly successful *Bellingham Mariners - A Bite of Baseball,* which enjoys continued sales. It features favorite recipes from former players, managers, coaches, staff and fans of the Bellingham Mariner Baseball Club and even the famous San Diego Chicken! (Note: The Bellingham team is now the Class A affiliate of the San Francisco Giants.)

It is Janet's love for cooking that has prompted her to create another cook book. These recipes, whether contributed or her own, feature the delectable fruits, flavorful vegetables and juicy berries found here in the great state of Washington. Included, of course, are many recipes for preparing the tantalizing seafoods garnered from our Pacific shores.

She urges her readers to "add your own personal touches" to these recipes and advises, "Cooking need not be a chore, it should be fun! Especially if you let others help in the preparation. These recipes have been enjoyed in my kitchen, and they will be savored in yours, too!"

More Cook Books by Golden West Publishers

CHRISTMAS IN WASHINGTON COOK BOOK

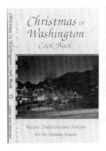

A sleigh full of Christmas traditions, festivals and treasured recipes from the Pacific Northwest. Many cooks, chefs, and innkeepers share their favorite holiday dishes including *Egg Nog Cranberry Salad, Moushella, Chicken & Herb Dumplings, Double Layered Pumpkin Pie* and more! By **Janet Walker.**

5 1/2 x 8 1/2—112 pages . . . $9.95

OREGON COOK BOOK

Over 200 great recipes from the beautiful state of Oregon! Tasty treats from the kitchens of dignitaries, homemakers, Bed-and-Breakfasts and author **Janet Walker** *(Washington Cook Book, Idaho Cook Book).* Sample the flavors of Oregon with *Hazelnut Stuffed Chicken Breast, Tillamook Seafood & Cheese Linguine* and *Earthquake Cake!* Includes interesting Oregon facts and festivals.

5 1/2 x 8 1/2 — 128 Pages . . . $6.95

BERRY LOVERS COOK BOOK

Over 120 delicious recipes featuring flavorful and nutritious berries! Try *Blueberry Buttermilk Muffins, Strawberry Peach Meringue Pie, Raspberry Dream Bars, Blackberry Summer Salad* or *Boysenberry Mint Frosty* and many more. Tempting recipes for all occasions. Includes berry facts and trivia!

5 1/2 x 8 1/2 — 96 pages . . . $6.95

APPLE LOVERS COOK BOOK

Celebrating America's favorite—the apple! 150 recipes for main and side dishes, appetizers, salads, breads, muffins, cakes, pies, desserts, beverages and preserves, all kitchen-tested by Shirley Munson and Jo Nelson.

5 1/2 x 8 1/2 — 120 Pages . . . $6.95

VEGGIE LOVERS COOK BOOK

Vegans will love these no cholesterol, no animal fat recipes! Over 200 nutritious, flavorful recipes by Chef Morty Star. Includes a foreword by Dr. Michael Klaper. Nutritional analyses for each recipe to help you plan a healthy diet.

5 1/2 x 8 1/2 — 128 pages . . . $6.95

ORDER BLANK

GOLDEN WEST PUBLISHERS

 4113 N. Longview Ave. • Phoenix, AZ 85014

www.goldenwestpublishers.com • **1-800-658-5830** • FAX 602-279-6901

Qty	Title	Price	Amount
	Apple Lovers Cook Book	**6.95**	
	Berry Lovers Cook Book	**6.95**	
	Best Barbecue Recipes	**6.95**	
	California Country Cook Book	**6.95**	
	Chili-Lovers Cook Book	**6.95**	
	Chip and Dip Lovers Cook Book	**6.95**	
	Christmas In Washington Cook Book	**9.95**	
	Citrus Lovers Cook Book	**6.95**	
	Easy RV Recipes	**6.95**	
	Easy Recipes for Wild Game & Fish	**6.95**	
	Idaho Cook Book	**6.95**	
	Joy of Muffins	**6.95**	
	Oregon Cook Book	**6.95**	
	Pecan Lovers Cook Book	**6.95**	
	Quick-n-Easy Mexican Recipes	**6.95**	
	Recipes for a Healthy Lifestyle	**6.95**	
	Salsa Lovers Cook Book	**6.95**	
	Tequila Cook Book	**7.95**	
	Veggie Lovers Cook Book	**6.95**	
	Washington Cook Book	**6.95**	
Shipping & Handling Add ▥▶	U.S. & Canada	$3.00	
	Other countries	$5.00	

☐ My Check or Money Order Enclosed $

☐ MasterCard ☐ VISA ($20 credit card minimum)

(Payable in U.S. funds)

Acct. No.	Exp. Date
Signature	
Name	Telephone
Address	
City/State/Zip	

Call for a FREE catalog of all of our titles

11/01 **This order blank may be photocopied** Wash Ck Bk